Jonathan Power

When Are You Going to Get a Proper Job?
Sixty Years in Journalism

The World Was My Oyster

Jonathan Power

WHEN ARE YOU GOING TO GET A PROPER JOB?

SIXTY YEARS IN JOURNALISM

The World Was My Oyster

Edition Noëma

Bibliographic information published by the Deutsche Nationalbibliothek
Die Deutsche Nationalbibliothek lists this publication in the Deutsche Nationalbibliografie; detailed bibliographic data are available on the Internet at http://dnb.d-nb.de.

Bibliografische Information der Deutschen Nationalbibliothek
Die Deutsche Nationalbibliothek verzeichnet diese Publikation in der Deutschen Nationalbibliografie; detaillierte bibliografische Daten sind im Internet über http://dnb.d-nb.de abrufbar.

Cover: Foto 36688220 © Robert Hyrons | Dreamstime.com

ISBN (Print): 978-3-8382-1838-0
ISBN (E-Book [PDF]): 978-3-8382-7838-4
© *ibidem*-Verlag, Hannover • Stuttgart 2024

Printed in the United States of America

For my children, grandchildren, sister, nieces and nephew, and Anne and Jeany— and those to come.

Also grateful thanks to my editor, Jessica Haunschild, for a job well done.

"We will never have peace in the world until men everywhere recognise that ends are not cut off from means, because the means represent the ideal in the making, and the end in process, and ultimately you can't reach good ends through evil means, because the means represent the seed and the end represents the tree."

Martin Luther King

Table of Contents

Chapter 1
I and Me

My life would have been so good — if only I had been more lucky, wise, sensible, stable — use any adjective you want. It did not happen the way I wanted. I never found the clarity of mind, the right sound or perfect female. I died with no money in the bank. I had nothing I had written that I wanted to pass on to the next generation. In love I had failed time and time again. In truth my life was long — I'm 83 — but I had nothing much to say. My father often asked, "When are you going to get a proper job?" From his perspective, as a free-lance journalist with a family, on a low income, I was wasting my life away. He said I would end up in a dusty room, looking at a naked lightbulb.

Don't be so bleak, I told my inner self. All this is not true. You are twisting the facts. You *have* done well. And the pursuit of love has had its successes, as well as momentous failures. You must have had a bad night — or a bad day. At least true in part, I answer back, but then I had high ambitions. "A man's reach must exceed his grasp or what are heavens for?" wrote the Scottish poet, Robert Browning.

My life was by no means pure when at fourteen years old I prayed on my knees for the first time in a serious way. But I did, instinctively, lean towards goodness and justice. Christianity, adopted during a wonderful summer in a boys' camp on the Welsh Island of Anglesey, run by a Baptist preacher, exploited that yearning very well, offering also a bonus with its promise of eternal life.

In life I didn't find the perfect human being — although I met some great ones in my life — Martin Luther King (for whom I worked in Chicago's black West Side ghetto), his closest aides, Andy Young and Jesse Jackson, (both long-time friends who I regularly talk to), Nigerian president, Olusegun Obasanjo (a friend for over 40 years), Julius Nyerere, president of Tanzania, Mahub ul Haq, finance minister of Pakistan, Sartaj Aziz, foreign minister of Pakistan, Buddy Weiss, my first editor at the International Herald Tribune who gave me the greatest break of my life and at the tender age of 33 made me a foreign affairs columnist and commentator—which I was for 17 years, Jim Grant, the head of UNICEF who along with Barbara Ward, the great political and economics writer, liked to mentor me and make sure I had enough money to live on when the International Herald Tribune would only pay me peanuts, and Valeria Rezende, my nun friend and one time near-lover from Brazil who spent most of her adult life working with the poor in Brazil and ten years ago became the author of two novels that both won Brazil's top prize for literature.

I found some good women including two very loving wives, one of whom, Anne, was my partner in working on Martin Luther King's staff and afterwards living and working in a Dickensian neighbourhood in London. She taught me how to write and backed me up with my journalism, even though she wasn't very taken by the media. She rather despised its bias towards simplifying and dramatizing too much, and its rather rightward political leanings, especially its bias against Russia and China. We shared the essential social and political ideas over the 20 years of our relationship. She is a workaholic—the poor of Britain rarely have had such an intelligent and strong-willed champion. Enormously kind and generous too. She started in London organizing playgroups for poor mothers and their children, went on to develop housing coops on the model I'd recommended in Chicago and eventually became a professor at the London School of Economics. We had three children.

I was faithful to Anne for 20 years, (we were boyfriend and girlfriend for three years before we married), until I met Mary Jane, a stewardess on an American Airlines plane flying from Jamaica to New York. After months of continuous travel from one end of the world to the other that year, in which I was often very lonely, (the foreign correspondent's lot) I took her to dinner, and before the evening was out she invited me to bed. I refused but promised to see her again on my next trip to New York. We went to Jamaica where I wanted to write about the volatile political situation. The seduction worked. I was caught up in her femininity — the marvelous figure, the bikini she wore on the beach, the flimsy way she dressed, her dress ruffled beguilingly by the gentle tropical breeze.

Mary Jane lived in New York and Oklahoma but seemed to prefer being up in the sky than with me. Her main accomplishment, looking back, was that unlike most southerners she was totally non-racist. At the end, after our breakup, she lied to the judge in our contest for the possession of the houseboat I owned on the Thames in Chelsea. (My daughter's second name is Chelsea, so attached was I to the boat I'd rescued from the knacker's yard.) But she wrenched it off me.

Anne had a multitude of virtues but making an effort to look feminine was not one of them. Over the years that had irritated me more and more. Despite all my encouragement she wouldn't change, and it gradually sapped the sexuality out of me. The problem was compounded by the fact that the beginning of our sex life only began on the day we were married. For the three previous years I had had to suffer Anne's Catholic fundamentalist morality which only allowed, she maintained, kisses on the cheek. So, on our marriage day when the green flag was hoisted, I couldn't do "it" for the first few days. That gave me a sexual nervousness that has lasted on and off all my subsequent life.

We had three lovely daughters and it grieved me more than I can ever write that she made it so very difficult for them to see me. I refused to go to court about anything. I gave her the house lock, stock, and barrel. I refused to legally fight for access to the children hoping that she would ameliorate her stance, but she never did. Above all, I wanted to avoid a bitter confrontation, not least for the children's sake.

I was badly torn but in the end I chose the pull of femininity and sex. I thought I could not go through life without passion. I'd read about it in novels and seen it on film and in the theatre and opera house. I had to experience it — the great, luring, overpowering, unknown. Yet to leave Anne and my children pushed me into a profound depression, the deepest one of my life. Only when, after three weeks of damning indecision, I decided in desperation to cross the Atlantic to Mary Jane did the depression lift—within an hour of the plane leaving Heathrow. I had felt I was in a dark pit with no way to escape. I realized my religious belief had deserted me—the very thing that should have saved both me and my family. I was crucified by what I was doing to my girls. Can the urge for good sex overwhelm all other feelings? Apparently, it can and I know I'm not the only one, although, praise to God, 90% of mothers and fathers would never do what I did and leave their children to cross the Atlantic and live there, if only half time, once I had bought my house boat on the Thames in Chelsea. No wonder nearly all my friends deserted me. It took me 20 years to recover from my feeling of profound guilt. In the end my eldest daughter, Carmen, pulled me out of it—well, most of the way. The guilt still lingers on. I know I did evil.

My second wife was Jeany, a successful Swedish opera singer based in Germany for many years, the country of opera. The relationship in its first phase lasted 17 years. We have one daughter, Jenny. Jeany not only has a voice to dream about and has performed all over Germany in its major opera houses, she is a great actress and a very warm, gentle, self-effacing and caring wife and hands-on mother. Although divorced—the Alfia story which I'll come to—we get closer and closer as the years pass and do a lot of things together. Twice a week we have dinner with Jenny and that is the best thing of all. Now she has Alzheimer's. Along with Jenny I care for her. Recently she moved into my flat so I can look after her more easily. More about Jeany later.

Luckily, unlike in London, I have made good friends here in Lund, an ancient university town from where King Canute lorded it over my country. They are mainly non-Swedish—the reserved Swedes are difficult to make friends with—although paradoxically some of my best friends are Swedish—I welcomed their tolerance in matters personal and the support they gave me when the tears were gushing from my eyes.

12

I often wish I could meet up with a handful of friends I've stayed close to over 40 years. I see them rarely since they are scattered around the globe. I feel a special affection for Peggy, the widow of Buddy Weiss, the late editor of the Herald Tribune. (What sizzling, drunken, conversations we had in the bars and restaurants of Paris waiting for Buddy to put the paper to bed at midnight!) I could also add Paul McCartney and my former editor at the intellectuals' magazine, Prospect, David Goodhart, who I occasionally see for a catch-up chat. And Chris Holmes who died too young who worked with Anne in the slums of Holloway and then became a very dynamic director of Shelter, the powerful housing advocacy group. When I decided the first time (there were two occasions) to break up with Mary Jane I went to live with my widowed father in Boars Hill, up above Oxford. An old acquaintance from my early BBC radio days, the professor of international relations, Adam Roberts and his wife Prinkey, took pity on me, I think, and often invited me for dinner which sometimes included a long run. We returned the dinners when Jeany, Jenny and I later moved to Oxford. We share a common interest in non-violent solutions to conflict.

Jenny Barraclough has to get a very special mention. She and I were a great team at BBC TV making pathbreaking documentaries about Black America. Together we won the silver medal at the Venice Film Festival. I was the reporter, she was the director. She is widely regarded as one of the BBC's great documentary-makers and won a BAFTA and numerous other awards. She taught me everything I know about filmmaking. More than that she was a great family friend and took it badly when I left Anne. For her part, in a BBC interview she singled me out as one of the most important influences in her life. Jenny continues to read everything I send her and often praises me for a particular column. Her enthusiasm for how well written my novel was helped keep me going as the rejection letters piled up.

I've written a lot, circa 2,500 articles and 13 books. (See my website: jonathanpowerjournalist.com.) Probably I'm the European who has written the most often for the most influential American papers—the International Herald Tribune, the New York Times, the Washington Post, the Boston Globe, the Miami Herald and the Los Angeles Times, (but not the Wall Street Journal owned by the corrupt Rupert Murdoch).

I've also written for the London Times, the Guardian, the Observer, the Sunday Times and the Economist, as well as the British intellectual monthlies, Encounter and Prospect magazines. Also European magazines and newspapers, from Spain's El Pais, to Germany's Die Zeit and Russia's premier foreign policy magazine, Global Affairs.

I've had influence on the presidents of the United States, Tanzania and Nigeria as well as on UNICEF, the International Institute for Strategic Studies, the World Council of Churches and on the UN's Security Council. And, I presume, for 17 years with my weekly column on foreign affairs, the readers of the International Herald Tribune, a paper that justifiably liked to think, with its excellent high-powered reporting and editorializing together with printing plants all over the world, it reached the elite of Europe and Asia (and to a lesser extent Africa and Latin America). Presidents and prime ministers read it with their breakfast.

I've always argued for charity, love, non-violence, justice, human rights and the end of racism, war and poverty—many of them subjects most newspaper editors—with the notable exception of Buddy Weiss are not particularly interested in, especially if the columnist goes on about these themes week in week out.

In love, as I inferred, I've had some successes and some failures— "Better to have loved and lost than never have loved at all!" I've had some wonderful companionship, especially from my wives. I've produced four girls, Carmen who has just finished her PhD and is an expert on the impact of birth upon the baby, Miriam, a swimming instructor who tutors in Lanzarote and has regular clients from all over Europe, and Lucy who, a first class degree in her back pocket, with her husband runs a program (Rowanbank) to introduce small children from low-income communities in Scotland and elsewhere to the joys of the forest and the need to tackle the phenomenon of global warming, plus their offspring, my quite amazing and loving grandchildren, Jasmine, Sophie, Lucia, Isabella and Isla Rose, all very different but all good members of humanity with superior talents. (For starters, the oldest, Jasmine (Jazzy Power), has launched a startlingly promising singing career, mainly jazz and folk — Paul McCartney has praised her voice. The second, Sophie, gained a first class degree at the University of Sussex.)

With Jeany I had Jenny, who after completing a year in her first job at the university hospital in Lund, preparing a website for the department dealing with arthritis, now copywrites for one of Sweden's largest travel companies. She is widely admired for the quality of her English prose.

The four daughters, I think, perhaps too proudly, are all recognizable chips off my old block. I'm very, very proud of what each of them has achieved. They all love each other. Not least is my kind and caring sister, Judy, living in Dublin. Over the years we have got closer and sometimes I have had to lean on her for advice.

Most of my current close friends are women, scattered around the world — Mathia, two Peggys, Mary, Indira, Kemi, Jessica, Jenny, Olga, two Karins, Lindsay, Valeria, Negar, Kyriaki, Kushi, Patricia, Barbara, Myrna, Cheryl, Paromita and my friends (half women) at the book club and the musicians at Cyrus restaurant. (Of all these only four are Swedish and the Swedish ones have all lived abroad.) I do have men friends, some of whom I've mentioned in the text above, but only three here in Lund

Alfia is not on that list. My break-up with Jeany was finally triggered by Alfia. But after three years of tolerating her bad temper and violence the curtain came down.

I had no idea at that moment what Alfia was thinking about "the other man". When I went to see her, three days after she sent me an email and gave me her news, she shouted at me, "I am fucking him". "I hate you", Alfia, the Tatar, said again and again. She then hit me over the head with the French drawing I had brought her, shattering the glass and bloodying my forehead. (I had left her weeks before after many other assaults, some worse than this, but for two or three months I half regretted it and was, paradoxically, profoundly hurt and jealous when she found another man.)

Every morning for three weeks I woke up with her sordid lines in my head.

I must tell you a bit about Alfia's Tatar ancestry. The Oxford dictionary defines Tatar in two ways. 1) a group of Central Asian peoples including Moguls and Turks, now living in Russia. 2) a violent-tempered or intractable person. She was both 1 and 2. She was a spitting cat sometimes. Once after a New Year's party which we had left she started beating me for reasons I could never understand. Little in stature but possessed with the strength of a mad woman she beat me for a good 600 meters as I walked fast towards my flat and she tore my thick, mohair, coat into pieces. So I decided to turn tail and run back to my hostess at the party, knowing if I continued home she would force herself inside. Alfia, hot on my heels, pushed herself inside my friend's house, grabbed a large jug of cold water and poured it over me. My friend distracted her by getting one of the men to ask her to dance and smuggled me out of the back door and I ran home. Ten minutes later Alfia was trying to bang my flat's door down. At three a.m. she phoned me to apologise, to tell me how much she loved me and asked me to take her to the psychiatric hospital. I told her to take a taxi. For the next two days I sat in a chair, hardly moving.

A few years ago I got to know a Danish woman, Linda. It was mainly a platonic friendship that filled in for my limited number of Swedish friends. We did get close, but it wasn't a normal friendship. She was like a bird, sometimes soaring, lifting my soul, sometimes diving as if looking for another fish in the ocean or dropping me on some protruding rock, sometimes just hovering, sometimes just fluttering her wings. It was disorientating and upsetting. I told her she was like the Scandinavian spring — sometimes the sun is out or it's raining, with dark clouds fast scurrying across the sky. We have now lost touch. She decided to push me out of her life. In retrospect I now realize she was just filling a hole until a man she could love came along.

Close to my heart is Luba, a Russian. She lives in Moscow and works as a producer for the rather good TV station RT ("Russia Today") that from time to time, despite it being a government-owned station, does broadcast critical reports on Russian foreign, economic and health policy, although it is caricatured in the West as a loud propaganda machine. I met her nine years ago when I was at a conference in Moscow and she approached me in the street and asked me to do an interview on Ukraine and Crimea. She tore into me with sharp questions. I was rather knocked over by how pretty and intelligent she was. Every time I go to Russia we meet up. On one visit I was asked to speak—only one of two Europeans—there were also two Russians speaking and two Americans—at the unveiling of a statue of presidents Reagan and Gorbachev shaking hands to mark the end of the Cold War. Gorbachev was meant to be there but cancelled because of not feeling well. TV cameras from all over the world, including the BBC, filmed it. Four years ago Luba and I went and had a sublime weekend in my favourite city, St Petersburg, arriving there on the sleek, silver bullet train from Moscow in almost half the time it used to take. Only Paris equals it. Besides having a unique grandeur including the Hermitage museum and art gallery, once the Tsar's splendid palace from whose balcony Lenin egged on the revolution, it has the best ballet company in the world, the Marinsky. Ballet is my favourite art form—so graceful and just simply beautiful. (Opera is second, which is how I met Jeany.) Luba came with her 7-year-old son, Danya. She's quite a bit younger than me so, unfortunately, a romantic relationship is not realistic. But for a long time, we texted each other two or three or four times a week, sometimes for half an hour at a time, other times just a quick one. I got to know her pretty well in our very honest and probing text conversations. We were supposed to go to St Petersburg again but the Covid virus messed that up. Then came the war and she wrote to me a text that I still can't understand: "I have decided I don't like you anymore".

What is the future? There are, I believe, some decades to go since I'm so fit, healthy and well exercised, surviving happily on a frugal diet, so positive and optimistic by temperament (a trait I learned. I was certainly not born with it), enjoying my work, loved by my children—the eldest, Carmen, just wrote on the inside cover of a book she has just given me for my birthday, "You are the best dad and granddad. Thank you for always being there for me and the girls". Jenny, the youngest, gave me a mug at Christmas, also emblazoned, "The world's greatest dad". Miri, the second, used to tell me she was looking for a man like me to be her husband and Lucy, the third, likes nothing better than for me to give her a long cuddle and have her hair stroked! I'm at peace and good friends with Jeany with her generous forgiving heart. (Anne until very recently refused to properly forgive me, despite my many pleas. Finally, on my 80th birthday prodded by our daughters and Jenny Barraclough she did write to me, although she still does not want to meet me.)

But death is a certainty. What will my dying thought be? I joke that I want to die in the saddle, making love and writing until the last moment. I don't fear death. I've had a good innings. If I have a soul, which I sort of doubt, I hope it might live on in my children for I am not convinced there is a heaven. I like the idea of my great-great-grandchildren reading this one day.

****

It had been a long time in coming but today it hit me as I ate the last dish of bitter, crimson, damsons from the garden. The old tastes, the old smells, the lane, the one acre garden with the great oak under which my father would sleep on a hot summer's night, the drive down to the town of Oxford from Boars Hill, past where Turner painted the dons wandering up from a college dinner at the university, memories of an even more evocative past age, down to the ring road with its pounding lorries, then along past

Sainsbury's supermarket, often stopping there, and into the town. Now all this was about to end.

We had bought boat tickets to Sweden—me, Jeany and our little daughter, Jenny. Everything was in the van, crammed full, furniture, books and all our stuff to drive it over to my Swedish wife, Jeany's old but un-lived in inheritance, a badly neglected house by the river in the untouched, pine-forested, lake-filled county of Blekinge.

I had endured for too long trying to pay the mortgage on my father's bequest, his beautiful house with the big garden where our daughter, Jenny, now six, played in a children's paradise with the boy and girl from next door, the children of filmmaker Pawel Pawlikowski, who besides being my (always losing) tennis partner won an Oscar for best foreign film. Every day for the last sixth months of living there I had pains in my head as if a needle has been pushed right in—the luxury house standing against the struggle for the money to keep the bank's bailiff from the door because of my inability to pay a quite high mortgage. Not only daily life worries seem to press, but in fact the shadowy, sometimes grim scenes from childhood. We just had no choice but to sell and leave.

We drove the van onto the boat at Harwich heading for the continent driving up north to a new chapter in our lives. Except there was a caveat. Jeany had said she would fulfill my wish of living in the Canary Islands for a while—but not too long—if I agreed to move to Sweden afterwards. I felt my back was against the wall. We couldn't afford the Oxford house. A perpetual melancholic, I wanted badly to be in the sun and by the sea. I "signed" her contract.

So it was then back to pick up the two cats and off we departed for a glorious year under the volcano, by the Atlantic, in a house in the banana grove of a small, untouched village, with time to swim off the rocks (no beach so no tourists), to write a new book on the history of Amnesty International, "Like Water on Stone" (published by Penguin), to learn Spanish and to get healthy in body and soul in order to flush out the accumulated tension and exhaustion

We had a very good time. Jenny went to the village school and learnt accent-less Spanish. Jeany kept her singing going and I finished my book. In the end we stayed three years in Tenerife.

I thought I would never have to honour this promise to a wife I loved and admired and was so kind to me, and nearly everybody she met. I thought like me she would fall in love with Spain. She never did. She was often irritated by the Spanish and their slow, sometimes irresponsible, way of life.

When time was nearly up we argued in our gentle way about it. I told her that I would get depressed in Sweden. I was always a melancholic until I lived in the Canary Islands—and there it disappeared. We had lived for three years in Sweden before (Jenny was born there). I hated the dullness of both weather and people. It was difficult to make friends with native Swedes and when I was writing I was shut up in dull rooms with not much light. I told Jeany that if we went back I would be depressed and maybe, I said, provocatively, without really believing it, our marriage wouldn't be able to take the strain.

She was adamant. There was better work for her there and the schools and universities would be better. As it turned out the Swedish school was much less good than the one in our Tenerife village. In Sweden Jenny found that she was a year ahead of her class in maths, such was the worth of our Spanish village's headmaster.

I did get depressed. Our sex life deteriorated to almost zero, my work became harder, I found we had little to talk about, and finally our marriage did break up. After three years of being in Sweden I started my affair with Alfia whom I met in the park. We had only been seeing each other a week when Jeany found out, thanks to Jenny cracking my email. Very un-Swedish-like she threw me out without more ado. I was homeless and had nowhere to live but at Alfia's, even though that's what half of me wanted—but not the other sane half. Not for the usually very broad-minded Jeany, the Swedish way of toleration when erring partners are usually forgiven. Still, we remained close friends and often ate together with Jenny and, in summer, went swimming together in a nearby lake. Two years' ago she was diagnosed with Alzheimer's. Jenny moved out three years ago so she was often lonely, and Alzheimer's makes it worse. I try and do something with her almost every day for a couple of hours to keep her spirits up. Jenny sees her twice a week and deals with her accounts and welfare arrangements — Recently I decided she must move into my flat. Jenny took over the family house, much better than her living in Copenhagen.

What is love? St. Paul, often a bit of a sour philosopher, wrote to the Corinthians and made a masterful, soaring, interpretation. "Love suffers long and is kind. Love does not envy. Love does not vaunt itself, is not puffed up, thinks no evil, does not rejoice in iniquity, believes all things, is hopeful about all things and endures all things." St Paul is probably writing about Filial and Platonic love. But the description also applies to the interpretation of good, giving, sexual love — Eros.

I first read that when I was 15 and have tried to implement it through all my stages of belief and now unbelief. Over the last thirty years I have moved from a strong religious bent to agnosticism. Not for me is post Emperor Constantine Christianity with its propensity for unrelenting and unforgiving war, "maturing" to the point in 1914 and again in 1938 (both unnecessary, avoidable wars, a theme I've written about many times) when opposing Christian nations with mighty industries and armies engaged in all-out war with each other. And with one other Christian nation using a nuclear bomb to obliterate two Japanese cities. Certainly not Judaism with all its sanctified, apparently God-given, commands to Moses to tell his generals to slaughter the women and children who stood in the way of the Jews' push out of Egypt towards the milk and honey of the promised land. (All recorded in the Bible's Book of Numbers.) Not Islam, even with its generosity, sense of forgiveness (mainly to defeated Arabs, Christians, Jews and Persians) and its belief in colour-blindness. Islam has been from the start under Mohammed's banner a militaristic religion using the sword to capture and subdue parts of Europe, North Africa, the Persian Empire and eastwards to the lands of the Moguls in present day Pakistan. To me, mixing violence with religion, as all three religions have done, betrays the values and principles they supposedly teach.

Nevertheless, I greatly admire Jesus and his teaching—against violence, compassion for the poor and ill, generosity both financial and in caring, and above all the sense of loving—"love your neighbour as yourself". If you want to know what inspires me today and every day it is his teaching, the Buddha's and the relatively modern-day teachings of Gandhi, Martin Luther King, Mother Teresa of Calcutta—and my beloved friend, Valeria, who you will read about in my chapter on Brazil. (The heart of this benign philosophy is best expressed in King's book, "The Trumpet of Conscience" (Hodder and Stoughton, London, 1967.))

******

The space probe, Voyager 1, reaching past the outer edges of the solar system and moving into interstellar space, further than any man-made object before, sent back photos of planet Earth. Our world looks like a pinprick of light, just as Saturn looks to us. How Earth will look now that Voyager 1 has left the solar system and travels further is only to be wondered at. Our sun will be a bright spot in a dark sky—it is a star and shines but we, its dull acolyte, will have seemingly disappeared, so small and insignificant are we.

Only since 2013 and the taking of this photo has it become quite so apparent how little importance we should attach to our planet and its peoples. Yet many of our religions point out that, in the eyes of God or the Supreme Being, every one of us is significant. Human beings take their own existence very seriously. We regard ourselves as the centre of the universe, together with those we love. Romantic passion which enables humankind to procreate and make our Earth populated underlines our sense of exclusiveness.

Our cities are regarded as monuments to mankind's endeavour. Our art, literature, sculpture, and music prove we have soul and profound imagination.

But we are unable to square our existence with the nothingness our galaxy and universe impose upon us. We are truly lost in the Milky Way.

Does it matter if we have fought wars or made peace, committed genocide or rescued people from death, sought justice or perpetuated injustice, prosecuted war criminals or let them hide in Paraguay, Argentina, Chile and Brazil, built good or bad architecture, damned the greatest rivers or rolled back the sea, built ships, cars and planes, invented electricity, mobile phones, computers and invented the Maxim gun and nuclear-tipped rockets? Does it matter that America dropped nuclear weapons and obliterated two Japanese cities or that Britain has conquered at one time or another 80 per cent of the world's countries? Does it matter that Japan disemboweled the innocents when it invaded China in 1937? In the light of our nothingness are these not much too?

Another question: If there is a God of the universe — and some astronomers are now saying there could be multiple universes — why should this God need to make us? We may need Him. But vice versa?

It seems we are an arrogant people, obsessed with ourselves and sure that since many of us need a god that God exists. It could be it is we who have made that decision, not Him. Or perhaps we are God's experiment — to see if He could create goodness not just stars and planets. Then clearly it failed. Maybe now, sad as He must be, given mankind's propensity for evil, He would welcome us destroying our planet as we seem to be trying to — with nuclear weapons and climate change. Then in a million or so years from now He may give it another shot on some other planet in another galaxy, of which there are millions.

We are left with the unanswerable conundrums: What are we for? What are our artifacts for? What are our love affairs and marriages for? Can we ever find an honest, science-based answer to these questions?

Not if we live a million years are we likely to—although I could be wrong. Well, let us say a thousand years. Certainly, many centuries. Perhaps the answer will come in the time of our children's children's children. I tend to think there is no answer.

Meanwhile, most of us Earth-dwellers try not to be arrogant and arrogate for ourselves the answers to the perhaps unanswerable. So, we just get on with the life we have: getting as educated as we can, finding a mate, rearing our families, tilling the soil or inventing and producing countless products.

What is it ultimately for? We truly have no idea.

Yet this is the only existence we know or are ever likely to know. Most of us try and make the best of it. And so we should, which should mean not enjoining war, war crimes, and crimes against humanity, thuggishness, destructiveness, criminality, discrimination, exploitation, and infidelity.

We want in our world, honesty, compassion, responsibility, love, fairness and justice. And good governance of home, nation and world. How many of us can put their hand on their heart and say they have never failed these ideals?

We had better get with life for all its faults and complexity. Worrying over the fact that we are less than a pin prick in our galaxy, much less our universe, gets us nowhere. We must give of our best, make the best, adore our world and its peoples and then peacefully fade away, our job of living on this quite insignificant planet well done.

Chapter 2
The Peace Women —
A Report from Ireland

Mairead Corrigan was 32 when I first met her. Until six months before her life was nine-to-five as a secretary in a brewery and evenings with the "Legion of Mary" and her family at home in Belfast. On August 10th, 1976, her sister's three children (8, 2 and 6 weeks old) were mown down and killed by an out-of-control-car driven by an Irish Provisional Army gunman. The driver was dead at the wheel, the victim of British army pursuers. Mairead was interviewed on the BBC and, with a passion that has carried her through ever since, she denounced the violence and death that had now caught up with her own family and pledged herself to do everything she could to end it. The seeds of the Peace Movement of Northern Ireland were sown.

Pages could be written about this woman—her warmth, her courage, her self-assurance, her gentle but quietly appealing good looks, her dedication to church work rather than to boyfriends—but one small story she related to me says more than another six pages would.

It was the day of the funeral of the three children. She took some red roses from one of the small white coffins, and she walked alone up to Anderstown to the house of the mother of the dead gunman. She told me she didn't know what she was going to say. She half expected to have the door slammed in her face. In fact, she found the mother crying. She told Mairead that she had been crying for three days. On the kitchen table was a tear-stained letter that she had been trying to write to Mairead's sister—an attempt to say she was sorry for what her son had done. I don't know exactly how the story ended. I was too moved to ask her to complete it. But I think it's easy to guess the way it was. For in Mairead's every look, every expression, is a total dedication to a commandment of Jesus which says, "love your enemy".

One more story, for it completes a picture that might otherwise be too sentimental. Coming home shortly after the funeral from one of the innumerable Peace meetings, she told me she saw two good-looking girls in tight-fitting coats being confronted by two well-armed British soldiers. She stopped her car close by to see what was going on. The soldiers were asking the girls to open their coats to be searched. The girls were protesting that army standing orders said girls could only be searched by a policewoman and refused to cooperate. The soldiers persisted. Mairead at that point got out and walked over to the soldiers and told them they had no right to search the girls. One of the soldiers, realizing who she was, quickly whispered to his companion and they motioned to the girls to go. As they walked off, one girl turned to the other and said loudly, "I suppose we should say thanks, but I wish I didn't have to say it to her."

There were two Peace-Women. Mairead's partner was Betty Williams, a quite different kind of person. Married to a marine engineer, she spent long months on her own with her children while her husband was at sea. She had something of the look of an energetic working-class wife who hasn't had an easy life. That was my first impression when I met her at a London press conference. Close up, the first impression was not altogether wrong; but there is another side, not least a quickness of mind that cuts through a lot of the rubbish talked those days in Northern Ireland. "Army withdrawal?" she replies scathingly to an English journalist's question about pulling the troops out. "But we have nine armies!" She treated some naïve campaign remarks of the American president-to-be, Jimmy Carter, with the same sharp tongue. As with Mairead there is a deep religious commitment (she is also a Catholic) which appeared to grow as the demands of sustaining the momentum of the Peace Movement mounted. She also had an infectious humour that lightened up some of the solemnity that on occasion tended to overwhelm their rallies. She could take on a crowd of 20,000 and make it roar with laughter. She is perhaps less secure than Mairead, not always so sure of what she believes, but strongly motivated to get on and get things done.

I arrived at her Belfast home to find her looking as if she had been in a car accident. Eyes glazed and wobbly at the knees, she was barely recognisable as the hearty, jocular woman she usually is. But she hadn't been in a car crash; she only had a hang-up. She felt guilty that Mairead found it easy to love everyone and said that she found it "bloody difficult" (especially when it came to the Provisional IRA members). So through a friend she had invited two Provo women to come round and talk over a cup of tea: so that she could persuade them that she really did not hate them but only wanted to change their minds. Their visit lasted a bare twenty minutes, and the last few minutes were spent outstretched on the floor with the women kicking her. She did not want to tell that to the Press because she was frightened she would not be able to control her emotions. She would only end up shouting that she did in fact hate the Provos—and what good would that do?

One cold day in winter I sat Mairead down in a steamed-up café and over coffee I got her to tell some of her story into my tape recorder. "On Wednesday, August 11th, I tried to console my brother-in-law, Jackie Maguire, on the death of his three children and said, 'Perhaps God has taken them for a purpose and some good will come out of their deaths'. Jackie replied that too many had died.

"Like all the rest, their deaths will probably be a nine-day wonder. Jackie was right that too many innocent people had died—and for what? I promised myself that I would do all in my power to try to prevent even one more death and perhaps in some way Anne and Jackie might find a reason for the deaths of their three little children. Jackie gave me the opportunity when he condemned the IRA and all their violence to the press on Wednesday, and then I did the same on TV. Where do we go from there, I didn't know….

Then I heard that this lady, Betty Williams, had started collecting signatures and was going to organise a rally the coming Saturday. I phoned to thank her and met her on Friday just before the children's funeral. The next day was the occasion of the first rally, with 10,000 or more joining to demonstrate for peace, with banners from Twinbrook and buses from Shankhill. Then on Sunday we began to get inundated with requests from TV and radio, and reporters from all over the world".

Their promising start was built on sensibly and quickly. First, an emotional march of 10,000, mainly working-class Catholic and Protestant women into the Catholic Anderstown and Falls Road neighbourhoods. Outside St John the Baptist school, where the three children were mowed down, the women prayed and sang hymns while a group of IRA youths jeered from a garage roof. Later petrol bombers tried to burn down Betty William's house. They were chased away by local men. This was followed a week later by a 25,000-strong march in Ormear park. The weekend after about the same number marched through the Loyalist working-class neighbourhood, the Shankhill-Protestants poured out of their homes and embraced the marchers. Protestant churches rang their bells. But on the way to the march, 200 howling women and youths, sympathetic to the Provisionals, had set on some of the Peace Women. Several were kicked and dragged to the ground. Three youths dragged one young girl around a corner and urinated on her. And on the same day a sympathy peace march in Dublin attracted 20,000 people.

In mid-September there was a spontaneous demonstration of Protestant housewives and shop assistants. A paramilitary group, The Ulster Defence Association, had hijacked and set on fire two buses. Thirty angry women blocked the road, stopping the paramilitary taxi cabs from passing. Then another group of over 100 joined them for a spontaneous peace meeting in the road. They blew whistles to attract each other's attention. The Peace Women's answer to the IRA women who bang dustbin lids to warn their men that army patrols are approaching.

In early October, the Peace Women were back in the news with a meeting in Catholic Turf Lodge — It had been called by residents because a 13-year-old boy had been killed by a plastic bullet fired by the Army. Mairead and Betty had gone to the meeting in an attempt to calm it down and to try and re-channel high emotions. Although there were probably a majority of the audience sympathetic to what they had to say, the press dispatches focussed on the anger of Republican women in the front rows. When Mairead tried to speak she was shouted down. Betty was hit on the head and collapsed. They all had to take refuge in the sacristy of the church for two hours before they could get away.

I heard criticism of this kind of meeting ("it stirs up a hornet's nest"). For my own part I always have thought they were right. Confrontation is both good psychology and good press relations. It demonstrates the tough rank-and-file of the Protestant and Catholic ghettos that the Peace-Women were not exactly "softies". They will, of course, never rival the real "hard men" and "hard women" of the Irish Isle, but undoubtedly over time this kind of tactic will undermine the narrow self-confidence of those who just "go along".

Besides these well-publicised confrontations there was a whole series of rallies that passed uneventfully with large numbers participating. Most of them hit the front page of at least three major newspapers, sometimes more. Often, they were the lead-item on the BBC, RTE, ITN and US networks' news bulletins. The latter rallies had the added appeal of Joan Baez's presence, and her diffident folk-singer style blended well with the Peace-Women.

I went to two: Trafalgar Square and the Boyne. The first led that evening to all the principles, their friends and acolytes singing to Joan Baez's playing in my smallish flat—so much for the "neutrality" and "objectivity" of the press!

That evening I had the chance to talk with the two women about the mechanics of the operation. And formidable mechanics it was too—an exercise in "devolution" that made the politicians with their close-knit bureaucratic empires look more irrelevant than they already were.

Each neighbourhood was responsible for organising its own buses. The rendezvous point was picked up from the newspaper or passed on by word-of-mouth. Four months after the first march everyone knew what to do—get on your bus, take your sandwiches and thermos, and make sure you are at the departure point by 2.30pm—which left the two Peace-Women free to do the interviews and keep the publicity machine ticking.

This was right, for without frequent appearances in the press people would have assumed they no longer existed—why else did the paramilitaries keep the bombs going off?

The buses themselves were splendid travelling islands of hope. I journeyed the 100 miles from Belfast to the river Boyne, just over the Irish border, with Mairead. Every time we passed a bus that had stopped, she would leap out of the car, board a bus, shake everyone's hand and swap bits of information on her foreign travels with neighbourhood peace groups. The buses were unbelievably cold. It happened to be the coldest day for ten years and the frost was an inch thick on the trees and grass. I asked some of them what they did to keep warm: "singing" was the usual answer, but a busload of nuns actually told me they had "danced" (in the aisles, on the greensward?). Needless to say, with our frequent stops we were among the last to arrive at the Boyne and everyone was already all lined up. We had to walk the length of the march with Mairead being mobbed by the marchers.

The march from our side, the North, was rather carefully timed to meet down in the Boyne Valley where the Protestant King William of England defeated the Irish in 1690—the march coming up from the south, from the Irish Republic. The two crowds swirled towards each other for emotional embraces. The Northern Irish column of the marchers was led by Catholic Anderstown (the Provisional stronghold) and Shankill (its complement on the Protestant side). At the head of the Catholic republic's column it was Drogheda, Dublin, and the Reconciliation Ireland programme of the American National Council of Churches. Joan Baez sang "We Shall Overcome" and "The Lord Is My Shepherd". Betty Williams spoke of the need to trust in God; Ciaran McKeown (their clever back-room boy and writer) of how "nothing is more political than an act of friendship"; and Mairead Corrigan movingly summed up the Peace Movement's message: "Let's say on the 6th December the Irish people began a new battle. A battle to replace war with peace, justice, hatred with love, anger with friendship, injustice with justice, people without homes with people with homes, unemployment with jobs. Let us dedicate ourselves to this new form of battle that can turn Ireland back into a land of saints and scholars".

I could hardly wait, such was my euphoria that I hadn't experienced since I worked on Martin Luther King's staff, to embrace her when she came down the steps from the platform.

The Peace Movement rarely spoke in more precise words than these, which was both its strength and its weakness. Its strength because some simple eternal truths needed in Northern Ireland to be said again and again — that there can be no justice until there is peace, not the other way round. Its weakness because politicians, political activists and journalists like to see a programme of "specifics" and, soon bored with admirable generalities, consciously or unconsciously, sought to belittle and undermine the movement.

So did the press. Even the Shankill march, perhaps the emotional high spot, was given only seven lines on the front page of the Sunday Times. The Observer, doing only a little better, gave it two short columns. But even to sustain that level of media interest is going to be well-nigh impossible. The Guardian's Belfast correspondent, Derek Brown, told me that the main reason why he led on the day of the highly successful Boyne march with the Londonderry bombings and only gave four lines at the very bottom to the march was "what he guessed would most interest his readers".

This reporting made me mad. It was going overboard. It seemed like the journalists had allowed their cynicism to overpower rational news judgement. Le Monde put the march in a significant spot on its front page. Why not the British press? Sometimes, while watching and reading media reporting in both Northern Ireland and Martin Luther King's campaigns, I've concluded there is a built-in journalistic bias to relegate the performance of non-violent human goodness to the bottom of the page. However, I have to say, I think some of them behave better these days, although the problem still remains.

I remember how Martin Luther King's civil rights movement used to muse about their own organization's inadequacies, and they always maintained that it was the "enemy" who rescued them from the doldrums. The press acted out the old adage: "If it bleeds it leads". There was only press interest when there was either a mass arrest, the police beating all and everyone at hand, a bombing or some other savage and senseless act of intimidation. When this did not happen King's star waned, and the press lost interest — as during the forgotten Albany campaign in 1961 or even at first at the magnificent Selma campaign. The campaign had begun to wind down, the demonstrations had become less well supported, less vigorous. And then, unexpectedly, Sheriff Clark unleashed his troopers at Pettus Bridge to give the marchers the most terrible beating they had ever had. This was televised and it rejuvenated the determination of the activists and projected the cause to the front of the news. Less than two weeks' later President Lyndon Johnson decided to put the Voting Rights bill before Congress. It was passed.

Talking to Mairead Corrigan, as I often did, I suggested that the Peace-People needed to dramatize a wider cause. I gave her examples from my days with Martin Luther King. King was adept at finding micro-situations that represented macro problems. He ran tightly focussed campaigns that highlighted the practice of a small town, but which had national consequences. In Montgomery, his first campaign, he led a boycott of the buses. For a whole year in that Alabama town no Afro-American rode the buses. In the end Montgomery's city fathers caved in, and the buses were integrated — but so were they in thousands of other towns, for the Supreme Court had ruled that Alabama's state laws on bus-segregation were unconstitutional. On the Selma campaign nine years later, where I marched with a bus full of people I'd rounded up at my university in Madison, Wisconsin, King organised the local blacks to register to vote in one little southern town. The crude machinations of Sheriff Clark and the local establishment to stop Afro-Americans becoming an electoral force put this insignificant town on the world map. Every march, every murder, every beating became an item of news and in the end the president himself was forced to intervene. "What happened in Selma", said Lyndon Johnson in his address to Congress, announcing his bill on voting rights, "is part of a far larger movement which reaches into every section and state of America. Their cause must be our cause too". And what every conventional liberal politician plus much of the media in America had warned King was quite impossible became the law of the land. "We shall overcome", intoned the president, as I listened on the radio. I had the shakes.

Little did I know this experience in Selma was laying the foundations for my career as a journalist. I was studying agricultural economics, intending to return to Africa to work with Tanzania's small farmers. But my new wife, Anne, gave me a child at the age of 25. This didn't deter us from moving to the ghetto slum of Chicago to work on King's staff but the sometimes frightening experiences there did convince my wife that she didn't want to go and live in Africa with a baby. I asked her how I was supposed to practice agricultural economics in London! I had to grit my teeth and think what else to do. Back in Britain I started sending articles to newspapers in London and literally knocking on doors in the corridors of the BBC's Broadcasting House, about the civil rights struggle in America. It was perfect timing. I walked through an open door both literally and figuratively. (There were no guards on the entrance to the BBC as there are these days.) Yet when I renewed my passport two years later, I still wrote under "profession" "agricultural economist"! To me journalists were voyeurs, looking though the keyhole of life at real professions – doctors who healed the sick and engineers who built bridges.

I saw from the beginning how sending the army into Northern Ireland by the Labour prime minister, James Callaghan, had not been thought through. There was no question that something had to be done on August 14th, 1969. The Royal Ulster Constabulary's (a 98% Protestant police force) decision to use Sterling sub-machine guns and Browning machine guns mounted on Shorland vehicles in an urban riot was one of the more obvious signs that events were out of control. Left to itself the situation would have flared to appalling proportions.

It seemed to me it was reasonable to ask whether troops were the right instrument for pacifying the conflict. Would it not have been better to have drafted in an emergency force of mainland police? At that time Catholic rioters needed assurance they would not be attacked, and the Protestant rioters needed to be assured of law and order. A large independent police force would have provided both. And this would have been achieved without providing the symbol the IRA activists (who still did not have more than the odd gun) needed to persuade the Bog Siders and Falls Roaders that they were now "occupied" by a hateful British military force of conquerors who had on and off been cowing the Irish for centuries, often brutally.

The army certainly was an occupying force in Northern Ireland and was a provocative element. The fact is an army force is too blunt an instrument for the delicate job of bringing peace to communities who live cheek by jowl with each other. It was not trained for urban neighbourhood policing. The army, of course, was a highly visible sign of a dominant British political presence. It worked to stifle the opportunity for local dialogue. Above all it poisoned the atmosphere. In the densely populated urban landscape the army appeared to be everywhere. Army, guns and barbed wire became part of the local architecture. What should be alien crept in and became every day and acceptable. Violence blended into the bricks and mortar. One role for the army and navy there might have been: to seal the border and to patrol the seas; to stop the nefarious gun-running that made the level of combat violence possible.

I could never "prove" to those powers-that-be whom I interviewed that pulling the troops out was necessary or a mistake had been made at the onset. I was pleased though when I met an influential Cabinet member, Lord Longford, a Catholic himself, at a meeting in London and could give him the International Herald Tribune of that day with my column on this subject. I saw him concentrating as he read it slowly.

I decided to investigate further this in/out conundrum. I found a number of schools of thought. I went to Dublin to talk to Conor Cruise O'Brien, a Labour party cabinet member of the coalition government. O'Brien had been a big shot in the UN, running its peace-keeping operation in the Congo at the time of the civil war in the 1960s. He was a famous writer. He used to contribute to Encounter, Britain's leading intellectual monthly whose editor Melvyn Lasky, who looked like Lenin, had commissioned from me an article on the Irish troubles. But O'Brien had pulled out of Encounter pulled some years before when it was revealed that Lasky had secretly taken CIA funds in the 1950s to keep the magazine afloat. In fact, the CIA had funded all sorts of "good" things indirectly including the London Symphony Orchestra in an attempt to help the West to stand up to Russia's world-class cultural institutions. To me the revelations were so much nonsense. Wasn't it better for the CIA to fund literature and music rather than spies? I chatted about this to O'Brien. To Lasky's delight O'Brien began to write for Encounter again.

"If the British were to withdraw", he told me, "With no assurance of a stable agreement between the two communities, there could be another Lebanon in the North, and it would be bound to spill over into the South". That was the essence of his position.

Whatever criticism he had of past tactics (and he had many, not least the way internment without trial—a sort of Guantanamo— was introduced), O'Brien saw the need for more of the same for the present—a continued British presence and an acceptance that the existing level of violence was going to go on for a long time. When I asked how long is a long time, a shrug was the answer.

He believed that in the end some kind of devolved relationship based on power sharing and working within UK structures would come to be accepted. "While waiting for a consensus everyone must sit tight", he said. As it turned out this is what happened but it took another 20 years.

He argued to me that any concession would only enable the IRA to raise its sights to their ultimate goal—a "united Ireland". The Peace People's movement, seen from the perspective of this kind of thinking, was but a useful stepping-stone to the day, yet long-off, when an overwhelming majority say, "enough is enough" and the IRA Provisionals no longer had a sea in which to swim.

The "Army-Out" viewpoint tended to blur with that of the independent Northern Ireland advocates. There was a period when some influential Protestants floated the idea of independence. It first surfaced when nine of the Protestant paramilitary groups announced that this was what they wanted. British withdrawal, they said, could be staged over a decade. They suggested that an independent Northern Ireland could be governed with Catholic participation in the cabinet—a kind of power sharing. The debate broadened when the Social Democrats (the Catholics' parliamentary party) passed a resolution to study the question.

What were its virtues? It put the Protestants in charge but without a British army to lean on. I assumed that once the possibility of reunification with Ireland was one step removed Catholics would stop hankering for a larger "Irish dimension" and would throw in their lot with the attempt to make their part of the island work. And it assumed that without the prop of British and Irish government involvement the rival communities would quickly realise they had to live together and that no one is going to rescue them from their own mistakes. Some went further and said after eight years of upheaval the Northern Irish people had developed a separate identity and that this could be reinterpreted as something of a virtue, rather than decried as a curse. "We have all suffered together"…etc. The argument gained added appeal if one made the

36

assumption that a) an independent Northern Ireland would "enter Europe" and subscribe to EU rules on democracy and human rights, and b) that any tendency to backslide could be countered as it was in post-revolutionary Portugal by the bait of West German foreign aid.

The argument against this was strong, I admit — the Provos might declare an initial truce, but would soon restart the civil war, convinced that without the British army to stop them, a united Ireland would be so much easier to attain. It would be impossible for the authorities to crack down on them the way the Northern Irish government did successfully. This would only lead in a heterogeneous society to the old problem of Catholic reaction and rank-closing. A Lebanon would flare……….

But would it? Lebanon was not really an exact parallel for all O'Brien's use of it. An independent Northern Ireland would have been different in three ways. It would have been established in an atmosphere of good-will on both sides, particularly if the Peace-People had taken up its cause and also made it their own. It would have come after seven years of violence which left the majority of people sick of it. The notorious sea that the paramilitary groups swim in would have dried up significantly. There were not the masses of heavy weaponry in Northern Ireland as there were in Lebanon. And, finally, there would not be outside forces supplying and backing the conflicting sides as there was in the Lebanon. One thing the Irish and British governments could have agreed on would have been to patrol with an EU force the Irish side of the border and thus halt the Provos's link with their friends and suppliers down South.

The arguments for British withdrawal and for independence could have been taken together or separately or together. Together that would have given added attraction to the independence idea. But even with withdrawal on its own, merely as a tactic to reduce the level of violence and to force the communities to realize they had to find a modus vivendi within the UK, also appeared to be appealing. It was difficult to be hard and fast about the withdrawal argument. I presented in Encounter as strong a case as I thought could be made for it. But I saw the risk and dangers and O'Brien wrote a long letter to Encounter refuting it.

Could an experiment have been in order? Why didn't the British, perhaps with wonted secrecy, slowly withdraw the troops from the Catholic areas where the Peace-Movement was most active and had most support? It would have been interesting and valuable to see if, as the military pressure was reduced, the identity with the Peace-People increased. If this turned out to be true, there would have been a strong case for reducing troop levels in a further area and even for withdrawing the troops to barracks.

All these years later as I watch the Scots, who already have a great amount of devolved power, debating leaving the United Kingdom and entering the EU as an independent country I give myself a wry smile. What was regarded then in Northern Ireland as a bit of a way-out idea has become a mainstream, almost a majority, one in Scotland. There has been no violence during the debate.

The Peace People did bring a glimmer of hope to Northern Ireland. They showed, as I heard Martin Luther King say, that "peace is not merely a distant goal that we seek but a means by which we arrive at that goal".

In September 1981 Marie Corrigan married her widowed brother-in-law. On Good Friday, April 1998 the leading Protestant and Catholic political leaders and the British government signed a peace agreement that for most of the time since has held.

Chapter 3
Return to Tanzania

I shook Tanzania's dust off my feet 30 years ago and looked back only in anguish. I first arrived in this former colony-a place the British never put their heart into—in 1964, just after independence. I was one of the first contingent of volunteers who lived out in the bush and happily did what we could for the new African socialism of President Julius Nyerere. Later, I interviewed Nyerere many times, both for television documentaries and the International Herald Tribune. The last time I saw him in 1979, we had sat outside his house on the Indian Ocean, both of us exhausted after a four-hour interview on Rhodesia (now Zimbabwe) and South Africa—he was playing an important role as an intermediary between the guerrillas and London and Washington. As the sun went down we sipped our wine and watched the dhows gliding in from a day's fishing or a trading trip to Zanzibar.

Forty-one years later, as I walked away from the presidential office in Dar es Salaam after my first interview with his successor, Benjamin Mkapa, I headed down to the ocean and reflected on why I had stayed away so long. Again, it was evening time. The women were cleaning the fresh fish on the white sand. The dhows were flitting landward. Nothing had changed, but everything had changed. Nyerere had steered the country into an economic hole, as he himself recognised before his death in 1999. It seemed likely then that most Tanzanians would live on a dollar a day as far into the future as anyone could see. Now my hopes were recharged. Tanzania, during Mkapa's ten years of office, has become a relative success story, albeit from a low base. Although still one of the poorest countries in Africa, with a national income per head of $290 compared to the African average of $490, Tanzania had been growing at an annual rate of almost 6 per cent over the previous five years (which soon went up to 7%, which means that income per head doubles every 10 years). Inflation was conquered on

Mkapa's watch. Tanzania was praised in the important Africa Commission report — Mkapa himself was one of the commissioners.

Mkapa stepped down two years later which led to an orderly, democratic transition. The opposition parties have a presence, but they were not strong and weren't able to stop the ruling Chama cha Mapinduzi (CCM) party's candidate, foreign minister Jakaya Kikwete, cruising to victory.

I first knew Mkapa when he was Nyerere's press secretary. When I asked him why he abandoned Nyerere's legacy to create a rather successful, if still budding, capitalist economy, he gave two reasons. First, he had watched Deng Xiaoping unleash capitalism in China and saw the country climb from rags to comparative riches. Second, it was the end of the Cold War and the western aid donors, in particular the Americans, the British and even the Scandinavians, were no longer interested in propping up a declining country just because it was pro-western.

Joseph Mungai, Tanzania's minister for education, whom Mkapa rated as the most dynamic member of his cabinet (he had been struggling to transform education despite losing nearly 3,000 teachers to Aids every year), recalls a story about Nyerere that rings true. On becoming Tanzania's leader, Nyerere called on Mao Zedong. Mao told him: "I give you one piece of advice: don't create a middle class." And Nyerere never did. Indeed, when I asked what Nyerere would say to him if he returned to earth, Mkapa replied: "He'd say I'd given away too much of what was in public ownership. And he would be upset that I had built up such a prosperous capitalist class."

Coming to power in 1995, Mkapa led his reformist mark on everything from tax policy to privatisation, from the bureaucracy to human rights, from political freedom to a free press. Of Nyerere's well-meaning but autocratic Christian Socialism there is hardly a sign left. As deputy foreign minister Abdul-Kader Shareef put it to me, as we sailed across to his birthplace in Zanzibar, "Nyerere was redistributing poverty... We are not anti-socialism. But before distributing wealth we must create it."

Nyerere was a Catholic idealist; never a Marxist. He aspired not just to replace white rule with black rule, but to build a society based on ujamaa, a Swahili word meaning "togetherness." Nyerere had a vision of village socialism, where tractors and fertilisers could be managed by village teams and used in communal fields, with the village selling and buying in from the outside world on a co-operative basis.

His ideas fell on deaf ears, for Tanzanian peasants were used to living on scattered family holdings and leading fairly independent lives. But Nyerere brushed aside opposition and tradition. He ordered the relocation of people whose families had farmed the same plots for hundreds of years. Some moved voluntarily, beguiled by Nyerere's rhetoric. Others had to be cajoled. Villagers were herded together and told: "This is your village site", yet often found no running water, decent land or roads. Later Nyerere admitted that even in his home village, Butiama, ujamaa had not taken hold, and it was gradually abandoned.

All the while Nyerere kept most of his critics at bay. His manner was disarming. He was often the first to articulate what had gone wrong. Despite his own western education at Edinburgh University he believed Westminster democracy was alien to a people who had long sorted out their problems under the shade of a baobab tree. He brought in one-party government, although softened by competing candidates in each constituency. And he was tough with anyone he thought was blocking Tanzania's socialist path, unsettling Zanzibar or troubling the liberation movements like South Africa's African National Congress (ANC), with their bases in Tanzania. The jails filled up.

Nyerere was most compromised by his Zanzibar policy. Even today, that tail—of two small islands—can wag the mainland dog, as Mkapa discovered. It is the one issue that could upset Tanzania's progress in attracting foreign investment.

In 1964, just after Tanganyika was granted independence, Zanzibar, also recently released from British rule, was caught up in an unexpected revolution. The African half of the population overthrew its Arab and Indian rulers. Nyerere, worried about their communist rhetoric, persuaded the revolutionaries to merge Zanzibar with the mainland. Tanzania was born.

It was a stormy marriage. The new Zanzibari leader, Sheik Abeid Karume, was a constant embarrassment. All attempts Nyerere made to moderate the regime failed. In 1972, unsurprisingly, Karume was murdered. Zanzibar's unsettled politics rumbles on. The African Zanzibaris still feel that they are not properly consulted and the Arabs are unhappy because they are no longer top dogs. The 1995 election was rigged. The election in 2000 was never fully completed. In early 2001 there was a serious uprising in Pemba, the smaller of Zanzibar's two islands. However, there hasn't been electoral violence since. The last election was in 2015, which had to be annulled because of infighting among the electoral commissioners. It was quietly re-run in 2016.

For now, the Tanzanian economy continues on course. Emulating its neighbour Uganda, where the economy has been transformed since 1986 under the stern tutelage of Yoweri Museveni, Tanzania has many of the ingredients for take-off. Most impediments are man-made, as they were in Ivory Coast, which grew for decades at 7 per cent until its benign dictator, Félix Houphouët-Boigny, died in 1993. Then, because there was no deal on his successor, factionalism tore the country apart. The same could befall Uganda, where Museveni rewrote the constitution so that he could keep on running for re-election. Only the democracies with firm term limits look promising for the longer term: Senegal, Mali and Ghana, with their steady 5 per cent growth rates; Madagascar (6 per cent); Mozambique (7-9 per cent); Botswana (7-10 per cent) — the world's fastest growing economy during the 1990s, and Tanzania. Tanzania's faster growth can almost be measured from the day that President Ali Hassan Mwinyi returned the country to multi-party rule, three years before Mkapa's election victory in 1995, and took the clamps off the media and parliamentary debate. Growth gradually picked up, averaging 4 per cent during 1995-99 and rising to an average of 5.8 per cent during 2000-04 and thence 7%. Alas, all these figures gathered before Covid, have had to be cut by a couple of per cent. (Interestingly, Africa had a lower rate of infections than any other continent.)

When at university I studied tropical agriculture the basic text was Pierre Gourou's "Le Monde Tropical". It was a sympathetic account of the difficulties of tropical life — leached soils, uncontrollable disease for humans and animals, either too much forest as in the Congo or too little as in the Sahel. Moreover, Africa's rivers did not have the fertile flood plains of the big Asian rivers, hospitable to paddy. It was a tale of woe that I used to explain to anyone who would listen why Africa would have the devil's own job of ever making it. But the progress of the countries listed above — and there are another 17 in sub-Saharan Africa which attained 5 per cent growth before the Great Recession of the US and Europe hit it — shows how inadequate this explanation is. For a start, growth does not depend solely on the land. These countries have shot ahead because, as in Tanzania, a combination of mining, tourism, small manufacturing and non-traditional exports such as flowers, timber, fish and precious stones have got them going. Agriculture, of course, has to come next — two thirds of Tanzanians still live on the land — if the growth rate is to reach 7 per cent and stay there — but the signs I saw are propitious.

Extensive privatisation of the large but moribund state sector has released commercial energy. For the most part it has been successful. There were a few cases of insiders getting control of productive assets at knockdown prices. And, as with the row over the privatisation of the household water supplies of Dar es Salaam, where a British and German-run company had its contract terminated by the government, it is difficult where necessities are concerned for public opinion to understand the needs of the capitalist to make a profit, or for the capitalist to understand the real needs of poor people.

I am returning to Iringa—eight hours by road from Dar es Salaam—where I worked 60 years ago. An hour or so before we arrive, the scenery begins to change from the endless, empty, dry savannah to the bold outcrops and massive boulders of outsize granite that characterise much of Tanzania's southern highlands. Seemingly wedged between the rocks are the small, brown, mud-built houses of what was, when I was last here, an impoverished peasant class. But now I can see that the green of the maize fields is broken up by a new crop, the waving, yellow heads of sunflowers, and the vendors beside the road are selling not just little heaps of vegetables, as in the past, but massive baskets of tomatoes and big cans of oil. Finally, the road winds up to Iringa, once a flourishing colonial outpost but now a bit tatty despite the fetching sight of purple jacaranda trees, a legacy, along with the rustic, stone-built local government buildings, from pre-first world war days when Germany was the ruling master. (Germany controlled Tanganyika and parts of Zanzibar in the late 19th century, and held on to the mainland until 1919. Both Tanganyika and Zanzibar were then ruled by Britain until the early 1960s.)

The state-run factories established by Nyerere were falling into ruin. But in the town's market new life was sprouting. Where before there were a few women selling a pile of potatoes or a handful of onions, there were now mountains of every vegetable and fruit: courgettes and guavas, cabbages and mangoes. There are beans and lentils, and fish from as far as lakes Tanganyika and Victoria. And everywhere those great baskets of tomatoes whose surplus pours into a new factory, making sauce. I found a new jam factory processing local fruit, and a cigarette factory using the tobacco that I used to encourage my dozen peasants to grow. What does it matter that the towering silos for corn are now empty? With their mobile phones—which cover 90+ per cent of the villages in the district—traders are finding their own immediate markets elsewhere in the country, or even in Zambia and Zimbabwe.

If diet has been transformed, so has health. There are 40 new dispensaries scattered around the district, with a couple of nurses for each, and half a dozen health centres with a doctor in attendance. The dispensaries help with childbirth and inoculations (which are up all over Tanzania) and a free supply of condoms. The country folk in Tanzania are still wary of birth control, but attitudes are changing—fertility rates have begun a slow decline and the health clinic I visited had run out of its quota of condoms. If Tanzania can get its birth rate down, the fruits of its agricultural revolution in the making will begin to show. But in a country where sex begins for most in their early teens and virginity at marriage is a concept known to only a handful of tribes, progress is going forward. But Aids does not help. Around 4.5 per cent of adults are infected with HIV. Still, neighbouring Uganda has turned the tide on Aids dramatically, so why shouldn't Tanzania? In fact, at last, it is making progress.

What is remarkable is that the Iringa peasants have done so much, so fast on their own initiative, mainly just because price controls were lifted and the market became their incentive. And in half a dozen other regional centres a similar story can be told. But Mkapa says he has neglected agriculture and that whoever takes over from him must make it a priority. As the economy grows, Tanzania has to feed its growing urban population. They will certainly have the buying power to give the farmers the incentives they need. But it is also a question of knowhow and services. The peasants need decent roads, a lighter tax burden for the agricultural sector, micro-credit and subsidised fertiliser (the IMF has at last allowed Tanzania to subsidise the transport of fertiliser). And they need improved seed—the sooner Europe withdraws its opposition to genetically modified seeds, which makes it impossible for a country that wants to be a major agriculture exporter to start using them, the better.

At the same time, Tanzania must continue its policy of attracting expatriate, professional farmers. There used to be small colonies of these—in the southern highlands and in the north around Arusha. Over the years, many gave up because the socialist tax and marketing policies hemmed them in. Now those that remained are getting a second wind—like the big dairy farmer near Iringa and the coffee farmer who is selling speciality coffee to Starbucks. Tanzania should, like Nigeria, welcome white Zimbabwean farmers. Land is still plentiful. Why not encourage European, Australian and American farmers to set up businesses, as long as they establish outlying subsidiaries among local peasant farmers?

What else does Tanzania have to do? Historically, its political stability led to it receiving more aid than most other African countries. Its debt burden was effectively halved in 2001 under the so-called "enhanced highly indebted poor countries' debt relief initiative," a move which should have saved the country around $3bn over 20 years. But this was superseded in 2003 when Tanzania became one of the 18 countries to benefit from the G7 finance ministers' agreement to completely write off multilateral debt—saving the country over $100m in repayments a year.

Does the country need a lot more aid? Has the debt relief removed a millstone from its neck? Is the much talked-about corruption really as bad as outsiders say? I posed these questions to Dar es Salaam's elite—to the shrewd German woman who represented the IMF, to the well-informed Kenyan adviser to the World Bank, to discreet diplomats, to ebullient Tanzanian economists, careful bankers, proud businessmen and reflective ministry of finance officials. Along the way I had a number of opportunities to bounce questions off an undefensive president and Joseph Mungai, minister of education, who once attended a class on current affairs I taught in Iringa. There was a strong consensus in the replies, even though the Tanzanians, flushed with their success so far, perhaps make the mistake of thinking that progress will get easier, not harder.

The future, in part, has to be more of the same—continuing macroeconomic discipline, more mining and more upmarket tourism. Tanzania is one of the most beautiful countries in the world, with wildlife parks, some in the south rarely visited, the 18,000—year-old rock paintings of Kondoa-Irangi, thousands of miles of safe Indian ocean coastline and, on its coast and in Zanzibar, a rich historical legacy including the remains of Kilwa Kisiwani, an African city of the 9th century and various Arab settlements from the 10th century onwards including the mosques and forts of the Omani colonisation in the 18th century. Dar es Salaam itself, despite some ugly skyscrapers, is full of tree-lined streets and pretty old German-era colonial buildings, and the mayor recently announced a plan to restrict traffic in the city centre. Mkapa agreed with me that tourism should go for style and taste and, in a country where Muslims dominate the coast and Zanzibar, decorous behaviour. That, instead of mass market tourism, is the way to maximise long-term revenues.

Tanzania is belatedly giving priority to secondary and tertiary education so that its woefully undereducated workforce can be prepared for the challenges ahead. Its policy of a primary school in every village and better trained teachers has already produced results: the primary school-leavers' national exams have a pass rate of 49 per cent against the previous 20 per cent. The country could move twice as fast if secondary education had not been neglected for so long and if Aids were not killing so many teachers.

And then there is corruption. Mkapa made corruption a central issue in his election platform. But the diplomats still complain about it. The Americans refuse to give Tanzania aid under their millennium challenge account because they say there is too much corruption. But this can be exaggerated. While corruption should not be excused, it needs, especially in Tanzania, to be put into perspective. First, unlike many African countries, the rot never started at the top. The state is not being bled dry by competing rent-seeking factions of the elite: all Tanzanian presidents have been clean and the country is relatively homogenous (it is made up of a number of different tribes, but, unlike neighbouring Kenya, none is big enough to dominate). Second, when one presses a diplomat to name names, the offences do not seem that serious – a minister fiddling with wildlife hunting licences here and, despite a modest salary, buying an expensive farm there. Third, tax reform and more vigorous monitoring have done away with a lot of evasion, and tax revenues have increased manifold. At local level, freeing markets and improving social services has helped. No longer does one have to bribe to get a child into school or a licence to sell something. Still, corruption remains a problem in the bureaucracy, and, despite all the promises, there have been few successful prosecutions. But, as the American ambassador told me, corruption is much more extensive in the US.

And what is the role of the outside world? The argument about western agricultural subsidies raging in the columns of the Financial Times, the Economist and in the Africa Commission report is too esoteric. Any deal made in rounds of trade talks in which poor nations make concessions on agricultural access in exchange for cuts in European, American and Japanese tariffs and subsidies would probably help, but would also be weighted in favour of the richer world. A better idea would be for Tanzania and like-minded countries to call the bluff of western countries and demand an absolutely level playing field, in which both sides dismantle all subsidies and tariffs over the next decade or so. Such an approach, cutting through the labyrinthine complexities of talks and negotiations, would radically shorten the time frame of negotiations. It would also open up internal African trade, currently frozen by protectionism.

Tanzanian farmers, under-resourced though they are, have managed to feed a population that has grown from 12m to 70 m in the last 45 years. Rarely in recent years has the country needed to import food. If farmers had access to an unsubsidised world marketplace, they could start to meet its demands too, especially in the age of mobile phones. And the same goes for most food-importing countries: show me a peaceful African country with functioning markets that cannot meet its own food needs most years. Of course, famine does strike when the rains fail, as happens from time to time in Tanzania. But, as in Tanzania, if there is reasonable transport and the markets are unrestricted, food will go from areas of surplus to those suffering.

Does Tanzania need more aid? Should it be doubled, as the Africa Commission and Jeffrey Sachs suggest? There is no doubt that aid works. The proof of that can be seen in both Tanzania and Uganda from the times when they were given little or no aid. Nothing moved. Look at both countries now and you can see aid projects delivering. Even the Asian tigers, with their undemocratic but capable "development" states, could not have got going without aid — the Americans put South Korea and Taiwan on the road to success.

But aid only works if the macroeconomic conditions are right and governance and management are effective. A good example is the TanZam railway built in the 1970s by the Chinese — then their most ambitious foreign aid project ever. At a time when the war in white-ruled Rhodesia had cut off Zambia's lifelines to the south, this aid project was a godsend, giving Zambia access to an Indian ocean port. But look at it now: decrepit engines, ill-maintained rolling stock, it takes three days to travel what used to take one. Now the Tanzanians are trying to do what they should have done decades ago: letting railway routes out on a long lease. Only with sophisticated management of the sort Tanzania does not yet possess can they be made to work as they did.

Aid today is arriving at healthy levels. The British are giving the most and no longer demand it to be earmarked for specific projects. Instead, most money goes straight to the treasury, so that the government itself has the responsibility of making sure it works. The Nordic donors, the third largest, are doing the same, but the Americans, the second largest, still insist on direct project lending.

The periodic announcements on debt forgiveness are a boon to a country that has been struggling under the burden of repayments. But Tanzania is not being held back by lack of aid or debt relief. What it needs is not lots more aid (although some could be well spent on infrastructure) but more surety of aid. I have seen too many aid projects in Africa that start well but then collapse after a few years when the donor pulls out, leaving the maintenance costs to be paid by the country itself, which has neither the money nor the management skills to keep it going. Former UK Prime Minister

Gordon Brown's idea of borrowing from future aid budgets for a big bang of aid was the wrong emphasis.

And, more than aid, Tanzania needs more foreign investment for industry, agricultural processing and infrastructure. Investment is increasing at a steady rate, although limited to mining and tourism. Diplomats claim that corruption is a deterrent, but businessmen dismiss the argument because investors know how to factor that into their costs. Only foreign investment brings with it the knowledge and skills to facilitate the kind of export-led growth that the country's planners pray for. The door is wide open.

If presidents can be as dynamic as the late Ben Mkapa, if aid donors hold steady, if rich countries open up their agricultural markets and, of course, if the world economy continues to grow, then Tanzania has a reasonably bright future. This generation of Tanzanians has learnt from the mistakes of Julius Nyerere (and his accomplices in the World Bank, the Swedish International Development Agency, the British Ministry of Overseas Development and journalists like myself). I think the Tanzanians now know how to keep their ship pointing forward. I would cross Tanzania off my worry list.

Chapter 4
My long-time friend, Nigeria's Big Man

We were holding hands, the former African dictator and I. We had climbed the fence while the guards weren't looking and had found a path through the forest, close to Moscow. Olusegun Obasanjo looked resplendent in his blue robe. I looked quite ordinary in my grey trousers and a white shirt.

We walked on, relieved to be away from the stuffy Soviet guest house full of former presidents, prime ministers and foreign ministers who didn't talk to us much—Obasanjo because he was black. Most of them didn't seem to know how to talk to an African or what to talk about. I even heard the chairman, Olof Palme, the rather left-wing prime minister of Sweden, say he would never go to Lagos because it was too dangerous. Me, because I was merely a journalist and their editorial advisor—some lower form of life even though some of us have more influence than a government minister and our newspapers often do.

We trekked on. We came to a village. The old men were playing chess. The young boys were fishing in the pond. I doubt if anyone had seen a black man before, much less one who almost looked as if he was dressed like a woman. Obasanjo walked down to the pond. He watched them fish. After a few minutes he gesticulated and asked one of the boys for his rod. Whipping the line fast over his shoulder he whipped it back right out into the water. "That's where the bait should be if you want to make a catch". The boys stared at him but seemed to understand the point he was making.

We walked on, hand in hand in the African way. That was the beginning of a long friendship.

He regularly sent me an air ticket to visit him on his farm in Ota, two hours' drive from Lagos airport. He was successful and rich. Some say he had got started with cheap loans, probably never re-paid, from the time he was president the first time in the 1970s. I doubt it because he has strong views on corruption, a pervasive disease in Nigeria. In many ways he is an idealist. He was a loud critic of the repressive dictatorship of General Sani Abacha, so very different from his own military government when he steered the country back to democracy, only to have it usurped shortly after he stepped down.

I had (and still have) an easy-going friendship with him. I learnt from him and I argued with him. Apart from politics we liked to talk about women. I could be a bit cheeky, and so could he. Once, to my then girlfriend's consternation, ostentatiously peering down the décolletage at his wife's gorgeous breasts, I remarked that he was a lucky man.

Obasanjo respected my journalism and always said he didn't mind what I wrote — a viewpoint he kept to even after he returned to the presidency a second time. I would have been honest about him anyway — I like to think I'm that kind of journalist. On my first visit to his farm I wrote about his confrontation with a farm worker who refused to do what he had ordered. Obasanjo took a thick piece of old wire he saw on the ground and made as if to whip him. He begged for mercy.

But then in the same column I wrote about how he was 5 hours late in picking me up. Driving to the airport he had come upon a car accident. There were six bodies on the ground. A small crowd of onlookers and two policemen were standing idly by. No one was helping. Obasanjo, then a private citizen but still exuding authority, ordered the crowd to help move the bodies to the roadside and commandeered a car to rush one of the dead women, who was obviously pregnant, to the hospital in the hope of saving the baby. He then directed the traffic for three hours until the traffic police arrived. The next day he learnt that the hospital had refused the woman admission because there was no police certificate recording the accident. "I should have done a Caesarean myself, by the roadside", he told me. I didn't doubt he would have, probably commandeering some peasant's knife.

On June 8th, 1998, General Sani Abacha, Nigeria's dictator, died in bed at the age of 54 of a heart attack. Three days later his successor, General Abubakar, let Obasanjo walk free from the jail he had been incarcerated in for three years. I wanted to be there to celebrate.

On March 2nd, the following year, I pick up the Financial Times and read the front-page headline: "Obasanjo tops poll in Nigeria". So my old friend is going to be president again. I must go at once to see him. Then I realize I have no visa and the Nigerian consulate says it takes 5 days to issue one.

I decided to contact Obasanjo directly. That for a country that hadn't repaired its telephone lines for 30 years is easier said than done. I try for days. After what feels like 50 attempts, I catch a polite young man at his home in Abeokuta. "He's never here", he says, "but try his e-mail". "E-mail? Do you have e-mail in darkest Africa?" I feel like saying but bite my tongue, reminding myself of the old adage: "The darkest thing about Africa is our ignorance of it". (Today e-mail is everywhere. Most Africans own a mobile phone and sales of them are the world's fastest. Half of all Nigerians have the most up-to-date expensive Smart phones.) I try the e-mail many times. Nothing happens. I try the telephone again. Eventually I get through. "I wouldn't come now", says the young man. "In two days' time he's off on a world trip".

All weekend I mull over what to do. I don't want to sit in London for another five days, waiting for the Nigerian bureaucracy to tick over. Last time they refused me a visa because I had a South African stamp in my passport. It needed a cabinet decision to give me approval, which Obasanjo, then out of office, engineered.

On the Monday I start telephoning again. The young man answers. "We got your e-mail", he says. "The general is on his farm phone". "So he hasn't dashed off on his world trip?" "No, not yet."

I dial the farm a few times and a voice, submerged in crackle, (these days the reception is usually perfect), finally answers.

"Hold on, I'll get the general." The man comes back. "Can you hold on for another few minutes? "Of course", I say, now starting to worry about my phone bill. "Jonathan, are you there?" It is Obasanjo. "I can't believe it. I didn't know if I'd ever talk to you again. How did you survive?" "Only by the grace of God", he says. I learn later he had become very religious in prison, writing three rather good books on Christian belief and becoming the unofficial chaplain to those in prison with him on death row. He also persuaded the prison governor to let him have a piece of waste land and there organized the other prisoners to farm it, producing fresh vegetables for mealtimes. For my part, I lobbied Chancellor Helmut Schmidt of Germany and foreign minister David Owen to try and intervene and get him out of jail.

I love that voice—slow, rich and kind—but I also know his other side: a man, although bereft of arrogance, who doesn't suffer fools; who, when he chooses, can intimidate not only with his first class brain, but with his massive bulk.

"I want to see you soon. I want to do one of my long, full page, interviews with you". "Well come", he said, "I'll get someone to meet you at the airport". I explain the visa problem and suggest that I should just come anyway. He doesn't sound keen on that idea—even the president-elect knows better than to waste energy and time arguing with the almost impenetrable Nigerian bureaucracy. "We'll do a letter to the Nigerian High Commission. Talk to Ad-Obe, my assistant. He'll sort it out".

Ad-Obe comes on the phone to tell me how difficult it is to come to Nigeria and that I should wait until Obasanjo comes to London. But my journalistic instincts were already triggered and I wanted to be the first to get the long interview, just as I caught Indira Gandhi two days before she swept back to power in India and persuaded her to give me two hours alone for The International Herald Tribune. I had no competition after that, not even from the Indian press. I explain this to Ad-Obe who says, "Nigeria isn't India—It's chaotic here."

So it's back and forth with Ad-Obe. I am soon convinced, unfairly I later decide, that he is a supercilious prat. How can Obasanjo know what his underling is up to? I suggest that maybe it is best to meet in Paris and I can fly back on Obasanjo's plane. Obasanjo is doing a one-day rush to see President Jacques Chirac. (The French always try to scoop the British in Africa, even in their backyard.)

"OK. Meet us in Paris". "But where? Do you have a contact in your Paris embassy?" "I don't know anyone there", Ad-Obe answers. The telephone goes dead. I decide to wait a couple of days before I try again.

Three days later I speak to Funmi, Obasanjo's helpful secretary. She tells me to call in the evening at eleven. With some trepidation at the late hour, I dial again. This time the call goes straight through and Funmi's voice is as clear as a bell. "Hello Jonathan", she says, recognizing my voice. "I'll put you through to his room. If he doesn't answer it means he's sleeping." A mellow, sleepy voice answers. "Where are you? Why aren't you here?" My nervousness at calling so late subsides. I am not the pain in the neck I had feared.

I explain to him again how I think I know him well enough to bring out his real thoughts and give him a platform to the world. "I want to talk to you too. Why don't you come on the 19th when I'm back from my African and Paris trips, before I go to London?"

It's settled. At 8am I am on the phone again with Funmi. She will meet me at Lagos airport tomorrow evening. "Are you sure you'll be there?" "As sure as Christ's Second Coming", she shoots back. How am I supposed to take that? I had forgotten, beneath the corruption and violence which have long overwhelmed Nigeria, how moral and religious ordinary Nigerians are. Away from official responsibilities where corruption seems endemic — in personal life, with family, aged parents — they live the command to be their brother's keeper............

.........The crowd of returning Nigerians surges off the plane. There are few whites, so surely Funmi will have no trouble recognizing me. There are plenty of people holding up cards with names on them. But mine is not among them and I obviously give the impression of being a bit lost. A young man rushes up to me. "I was waiting for you. My name is Paul". "Jonathan Power", I say, shaking his hand. "Where is Funmi?" "She couldn't come. Mr. Power, come this way." We walk past the luggage carousel to the customs officers. "Give the man 20 pounds", he says sotto voce. My jet-lagged brain slowly starts to wake up. Would Obasanjo, the politician who campaigned as the slayer of corruption, have a driver who asks me to dish the customs 20 pounds? The customs man asks me what I have. Then, as usual in Nigeria, he asks me if I "have a little something for him". "No", I smile. "These are new days. Obasanjo won the election". He laughs and lets me through. Paul is waiting, urging me on to his car. "Where are we going?" I ask. "To the Sheraton", he answers. But Funmi had said most definitely that I would be staying at the farm. I decide to play for time. If he is the legitimate driver I don't want to insult the first African I meet after ten years away. "I must change some money", I say. I wait in the queue at the bank. A few minutes later I see a large lady with a green turban, accompanied by a younger woman, heading my way. Funmi recognizes me immediately and I give her a hug of relief. "This is Abimbola, General Obasanjo's daughter". We drive off and I tell them of my encounter with Paul. "You're lucky to be alive", says Funmi. "These types rob you, knife you and throw you out on the road."

The traffic is chaotic. It's rush hour. The light is failing and the owners of the shops which stretch endlessly along the road light little lamps to illuminate their stock. There are hundreds of churches. I catch a glimpse of the courtyard of one. A circle of men are kneeling and praying. "Pray for me", I say to myself, as our driver steps on the throttle as we move at a quite ridiculous speed past pedestrians, children and goats, all the time circumnavigating the numerous potholes. I look at the crowds packed into buses, people battling their way home, hours on the road after hours of hard work, only marginally better off than the cripples on the street. And what is this? A man bending over, bleeding from his head. A woman pouring water over his wound. Was he hit by a rogue driver? They all seem to be rogue drivers, not least ours. He is the fastest of them all. This is Obasanjo's campaign Land-Rover and driver, Funmi says. The driver accelerates. There is nothing I can do, only accept that I am in another world.

I sleep well on Obasanjo's farm. I am fed well and surrounded by the sexual and religious banter of Funmi, Abimbola and their friends. Funmi whispers to me that I can have any woman I want. "Even Obasanjo's daughter", I ask jokingly? She nods. I decide that might not be the best move to make. Even though Obasanjo has had nine wives and 20 children he might not be as relaxed about that as I might like. I give her a pass.

At 11am I am rushed to the airport from the farm, accompanied by Abimbola and a couple of her friends. I'm dropped off at a charter service and told to wait for the vice-president-elect who will travel with me on a private plane to the capital, Abuja, to meet Obasanjo. Two hours later his entourage cancels. I ask an oilman also waiting, which are the safe airlines in Nigeria. None of them, he replies. The oil company always charters a plane for its professional staff. Pressed, he recommends Bellevue Airlines if I *have* to fly. By mid-afternoon I'm in Abuja. A town set in the middle of nowhere, it was chosen as the capital 45 years ago in an attempt to decompress overcrowded Lagos. Surrounded by little villages of mud walls and conical thatched roofs, it is full of non-descript modern offices and hotels. If only the architects had been ordered to take their cue from the villages and the rocky topography around. But Abuja has its charm, too: an absence of crime; a towering cathedral whose cross can be seen 60 kilometers away; a magnificent mosque with a golden dome, as large as Istanbul's Blue Mosque. (About one third of Nigerians are Christian and nearly half are Muslim. This is the root of much political tension. Moreover, with the country split into over 500 language groups unity is the ever-present conundrum.)

I met up with the Obasanjo crowd of intimates and campaign workers. At 9.30 pm we drive in a long cavalcade to the airport to greet him on his return from Paris. The presidential jet lands, the stairs drop and Obasanjo appears, draped in a deep reddish-brown toga. He pauses at the top of the steps, exuding self-confidence, and then descends. Obasanjo has always carried his authority well. I linger at the back of the crowd, a lone white face, hoping he might look twice. He doesn't. I have no choice but to propel myself forward before he gets into the car. He sees me, pulls me close and we give each other a brief hug. I feel constrained. Perhaps he does too. Old friendship though it is, he will not want to show too much affection for a white man in front of such a crowd, all competing for his attention—and for jobs. "When can you fit me in?" "Tomorrow at four" and that's it.

We re-join the cavalcade which, on reaching Abuja, does not break up as I had expected. We follow Obasanjo's car up the long un-guarded driveway to a large white house. "This used to be Abacha's house", someone whispers to me, as we slam the car doors shut and rush into the building. We walk into a large room. Obasanjo and his vice-president are sitting side by side. We are handed fresh fruit juice by waiters in white suits and bottle-green buttons, the national colour. It is plush in a nouveau-riche kind of way. So is the retinue of hangers-on, sliding from one conversation to another, elegant in gold-braided cloth and leather shoes. Obasanjo is reading his mail and ignoring us.

Abba, whom I had befriended in the car ride, a former press secretary of the last democratically elected president, Shehu Shagari, pushes me forward. "Show him that column you wrote in 1984", he says. I had written after the coup that the generals one day would have to bring Obasanjo back if the country were ever to stabilize. I pull it out and give it to Obasanjo. He reads it slowly "You were always ahead," and takes my hand. "How long do you need? Will an hour do?" "Not really. Perhaps I could travel back with you in your plane to London?"

I retreat into the crowd. Around one in the morning, people drift away. I think it is time to go too. I don't want to disturb Obasanjo again but, with Abba prodding once more, I call out "goodnight" and start for the staircase. "Jonathan", I hear a big voice. "You haven't told me how your love life is!" I turn and laugh. "Come and sit down and fill me in. I'm too out of date". The last time I stayed with him, 11 years before I was with Mary Jane whose vivaciousness Obasanjo found appealing. But the doubt and pain of leaving my first wife Anne with the children had been written all over my face — in fact I remained with my torn and painful thoughts for a good 30 plus years after the separation. He wants to hear more. I explain it all. "You were never lucky with women, Jonathan", he laughs. "But you are looking good, something must be going on". I tell him of my happy marriage to Jeany, an opera singer, and of our eight-year-old daughter, Jenny. He smiles. He is happy for me. "She must come and sing here". The ice is broken again, or so I think.

The interview starts well enough. Obasanjo talks about how he has been physically reduced by his imprisonment but spiritually strengthened. He has always been a God-fearing Christian, but this is a different degree of religiosity.

After about forty minutes, however, the mood changes. I am pressing him on his plans for privatising the national oil company, notorious for its corruption and inefficiency. His voice, usually soft, starts to rise. His eyes tense. "Why should we give away what no one has yet put a price on?"

We carry on but I have rattled him. Third World politicians, even enlightened democratic ones who enjoy nothing more than a good argument in private, find it unsettling to be challenged by journalists. I had questioned him about army excesses during his last presidency and about allegations that the funding of his campaign came from rich generals of the old order. But the question of oil and its misuse is the most sensitive of issues in Nigeria. He was annoyed, makes some remark to the effect that an ambassador is waiting to see him and "ambassadors are much more bloody important than this" and abruptly ups and leaves. I decide I have nothing to lose but to follow him calling out, as if nothing untoward had happened. "Could we finish it on the plane tomorrow?" "We'll see", he says and disappears. I decide to wait. I have a very incomplete and unmarketable interview, and if I get pressed out of the timetable by an army of visitors waiting their turn I might never get my chance again.

Twenty minutes pass and my spirits begin to sink. Suddenly Funmi appears, miraculously transported from afar. "The general wants you to eat dinner with us". I am led into the dining room, with about 20 people around the table, and plonked at the far end. I am clearly an afterthought; they are all tucked into their first course. "We've known each other for over 20 years", Obasanjo tells everyone and we launch across the length of the long table into a dissection of the journalistic art. It's a conversation full of laughs and merriment. Old stories told and scores settled. The company is bemused as we slip into our old repartee. "I get nervous when you raise your voice", I explain. "I was getting angry", he says. "Your question made it sound that you wanted me to give away my country. Anyway, if you are my friend I can shout at you". "As long as I can shout back!" "But not in public". And so we go on..........

.............Now we are airborne together, on the presidential jet. Obasanjo holds my hand as we talk. The interview is good. I have what I want. After the tape is switched off we gossip about people like Helmut Schmidt, the former West German chancellor, who he thinks the world of, and who I had met recently to talk about an international newspaper I wanted to start. "But he can be very rude", and then we chatted about what would happen to the Clinton marriage after he left office.

We talk about Nigeria. I tell him I'm convinced that if real progress is made in the next four years in restoring ethnic harmony between the three big groups, the Islamic Hausa, the Christian Yoruba and Ibo and countless smaller tribes, improving the economy and maintaining democracy, Nigeria will succeed and that will have a profound effect on the rest of Africa's countries. Nigeria can become another Malaysia. He concurs. "I feel that too. But will I live long enough to get it done? Perhaps there could be a coup. It could come from the military; it could be a civilian group. Even in my entourage there are people I cannot really trust." "Why do you have them around you, then?" "Because of politics. They represent certain regions or political groups".

Africa slips away. Europe beckons. I start to daydream. Obasanjo interrupts my reverie." Why don't you come and live in Nigeria?" "Why? "Then we could always talk". He pauses. "I don't suppose your wife would want to". "I'll ask her", I say. I am very tempted. Probably no offer like that will come my way again. Imagine being in the engine seat, right next to the driver, as the great locomotive that is Nigeria picks up speed – and we talk, talk, talk…….………

………………..Two years later I was off to meet him again and see what had transpired in Nigeria. My wife phoned me on the way to Heathrow and asked me to call her when I met Pierre Sane, Amnesty-International's secretary-general, who was travelling on the same plane. After my last near-fatal accident at Lagos airport she wanted to know that I was going to be in safe custody. I told her I wasn't sure I'd recognize him among 400 Nigerian passengers on a crowded 747 – it was eight months since my only encounter with him over lunch. In the event, he was hard to miss. As I walked towards the boarding gate I saw him on a bench, talking into his mobile phone, paper on his lap, an elegant African in powder blue shirt, pale yellow tie, dark jacket, immaculately polished shoes, brown leather briefcase and a rather expensive gold watch peeping from his shirt sleeve. I wondered how such an appearance would hold up in the heat and dust of equatorial summer.

He handed me a paper on Amnesty's mission to Nigeria. The "travel precautions" section was not reassuring. "Internal airlines have a high accident rate. Armed robbery is common on the roads".

Both of us worked most of the time on the plane. Sitting in an empty row in front of him, my head turned round as questions came into my mind. "I see from the program you've only got an hour with Obasanjo. Is that typical with heads of government?" "An hour is about right", he replied, "Otherwise the discussion wanders. I have a lot of points here", he continued, "tapping his sheaves of paper. And the Nigerian section of Amnesty will have their own points. But we must select the main three and focus his attention on those, otherwise it's just a shopping list".

"Does Obasanjo know what you are going to bring up?" I ask. "We've written to him and the ministers we are going to call on". He showed me the letter to the foreign minister. A good letter, hard but polite.

"I am going to focus on impunity. His commission looking at human rights abuses under Abacha is stuck. They've no resources and that's maybe because Obasanjo doesn't want them to go too far. To be fair, he probably thinks this helps reconciliation".

He passes me another paper—an Amnesty press release on the execution of Nigerians in Saudi Arabia. Saudi Arabia, it said, "has one of the highest rates of capital punishment in the world, and 10% are Nigerians. The death penalty can be used for a wide range of offences including sodomy and witchcraft". Most of the Nigerians on Amnesty's list were executed—usually by decapitation—for drug smuggling and armed robbery. "The Nigerian press gave a lot of space to this release", Pierre said. "So you issued it just before you left to warm them up?" "Sure", he replied, smiling, "it's good to have the local press in a sympathetic mood when we arrive."

"Do you find", I ask, "that just being in a country, chatting to the officials and pressure groups, has a catalytic effect?" "Oh yes, often it brings things to the surface. Or prisoners get out. But it can work the other way. I've just been on a mission to Nepal and on the first day pro-Chinese guerrillas attacked the police, killing 19 of them, and the police retaliated. Apparently, this was done as a statement to us."

We begin our descent into Lagos, flying over a great expanse of fields dotted with small villages. A river meanders through. But within moments the outer edges of Lagos begin. From the air it looks, at first, tidy with well-proportioned, solid looking houses facing straight streets. Then the plane dips and flies low. I see the rusty zinc of the corrugated roofs, the crowded balconies of the apartment blocks, the traffic pouring between them, crowds outside a mosque, long queues for the yellow buses at the bus station. From here I can't smell the garbage and touch the violence. But I know it's there, shimmering and moving between the quiet surface of the evening light. Soon we will be on the ground, in the middle of it.

Since the last time I was in Lagos, two years ago, conditions had dramatically improved. There were more health clinics, schools and water taps, the main roads had bus lanes to give them an advantage over the stalled cars and lorries. There were flowers and grass planted at intersections, trees planted along the very busy main road and, I was told, there was a steady lessening of robberies.

An efficient foreign ministry woman meets us off the plane. Pierre turns down her suggestion that we sit in the VIP lounge while she retrieves our luggage. It's almost tranquil in the airport compared with my last visit when Obasanjo had just been elected president.

It's the same outside. There is no "Paul". The waiting crowd stands well back, yet there are only a couple of police around. Two men step forward, introduce themselves as the chairman and section director of Amnesty in Nigeria, then step backward to allow a group of 20 or so supporters to grab our hands, take our photographs and bundle us into a nice red car.

The next day we landed in Abuja. I phone Obasanjo from an airport phone box. He tells me to call him later from the hotel and he will send someone to pick me up. At 7.30 pm I enter the plush presidential complex, built by Abacha. It looks like the campus of one of America's richer private universities: low buildings slung around expansive lawns, broken up with shade trees. It is—as I find with an increasing number of public buildings in Nigeria—spotlessly clean.

I'm ushered into the dining room which has a long table set in another of the nouveau riche heavily curtained, thick carpeted rooms which seem to be the taste of the military, to find Obasanjo sitting at its head with his entourage. He is reading a five-day-old Financial Times and I ask him if this is his daily fare. "No, someone just brought it in". He looks at what I'm carrying—Prospect and the new Ondaatje novel—and raises an eyebrow, as if to say, "Are these for me?" Since I have brought no present, I offer them up. Obasanjo is a voracious reader—and writer. The one of his three prison-written books that I have read, "This Animal Called Man", is an erudite exposition of Christian belief, and very well written too. We often talk religion—I the doubter, who wishes he wasn't, and he the amateur evangelist whose prison years made him even more fervent.

"So you are travelling with Amnesty. What do they want? I've got nothing to say to them", he says in the gruff military manner he uses to intimidate. "Is it Odi?" "I think that's on their list", I answer. (Odi is a town in Niger delta where, Amnesty said, the military carried out extra-judicial executions in September 1999, after coming under fire while arresting armed youths who had allegedly killed 12 police officers.) He shook his head. "It seems that executions are still going on here and there", I say. "Amnesty doesn't know what really happens", he comments, "So why isn't there an enquiry?" I push, wondering how far I can go before triggering his temper. I change the subject. "I think the other thing they'll bring up is this commission investigating human rights abuses under the military governments. It seems to be moving slowly". "They should go and talk to Justice Oputa, the chairman". "They will, but you told me last year that you were going to crack the whip". "I am cracking it", he says firmly. He turns to talk to another guest, the former governor of Lagos state under Abacha. Then he leaves the room without a word.

When he returns half an hour later I ask him what effect Amnesty had in helping to undermine Abacha. "It's hard to pinpoint. On the surface it seemed that nothing moved him. But all those pressures from the outside had an effect. There is much speculation on what caused Abacha's death at such a young age. One factor was stress from external pressure". He paused, "Amnesty is good, the world needs it, but they are not always right". (Obasanjo had been of one of Amnesty's best known "prisoners of conscience" for three years. Later, on one trip to London he went to their office to say, "thank you".)

I warn him that Sane is a tough act. "Some say he fires from the hip, I think he fires from the shoulder. Anyway, some bullets are coming your way tomorrow!" He doesn't like my quip. "I'll walk out, you know, if I don't like it". His anger flashes, subsides and the conversation drifts. He disappears and comes back in shorts and a t-shirt. "Come and watch me play, I do this twice a day". We walk to the squash court, and he plays a fast and victorious game against one of his staff. "You intimidate them", I say. "I'm good", he says, grinning.

At 3 pm the next day the Amnesty delegation and I arrive at the presidential palace. Mahogany-panelled rooms, marble floors and staircases — I wonder how many villages could have had running water or a primary school with the money spent on this. Perhaps this crosses Obasanjo's mind too, but whom could he sell to?

We sit in a rather formal room. Obasanjo enters. We are called to stand, and he sits himself with four advisers at the head of the table. I purposely sit apart. On the other side of the table sit Pierre and his staff including local Amnesty representatives. Pierre gives an introduction, careful to underline how open the country now feels, how the sense of fear has gone. "I realize", he says, "that democracy doesn't solve all the problems overnight; you have inherited massive human rights abuses. We are here to talk about both the abuses of the past and those which continue under a justice system that hasn't much changed."

He then runs through the evidence of continuing extrajudicial executions, torture, the abuse of women in prisons, and police behaviour. Obasanjo begins: "I don't have much time, but I want to say I have a high opinion of Amnesty. I've always commended your work". Then he picks up the ball and runs with it for almost an hour: he lowers his voice, raises it, tells anecdotes, firmly knocks back most of the Amnesty proposals, but says if they have evidence of torture in prisons then to pass the information on directly to him.

It was done with great charm, but on the essentials he was not to be moved. On the crucial issue of the behaviour of the army Obasanjo was, as Pierre put it, "thinking as a soldier". "You have to think about the morale of the army, yes, but you also have to think about the bad things the army does," says Pierre. "Have you ever been shot at, Pierre?" counters the president, who was shot at many times during the war in Biafra. Pierre shakes his head modestly, although I know his life has been threatened a number of times. "Unfortunately", Obasanjo adds smiling "there's nowhere where we can send Pierre to be shot at!" Only at the end, when Pierre raises the question of the abolition of the death penalty, does there seem to be a modest meeting of the minds. "Don't push me to run. I'm crawling, sometimes walking. That's how I want it". No, he would not declare a moratorium. "The trouble with moratoriums is that they come to an end. And it's a wasted opportunity if one has to go back. I want to abolish the death penalty. I'm working towards it, but I have a lot of educating to do. Even when I was the military president I did not sign any death warrants and I won't sign any now. But this is also a decision for each governor, so I can't interfere. But you in Amnesty must work to uncover miscarriages of justice, so the people can be educated to the flaws in capital punishment".

Pierre and his team have done their forceful and eloquent best. No one fluffed their lines and they knew their stuff. I look across at Pierre. I see his eyelids are heavy, almost closed. This is out of character. He hasn't won a point and it shows.

But walking down the corridor after the meeting they want to believe that some good has come from it. "We saw him and the door is open", said Pierre. "We can write to him and follow it up". "We have built a relationship, and there was no hostility", another says.

They had fallen under the same spell as I had years ago. Obasanjo is so straightforward, so unduplicitous in argument, with a manner so authoritative, that even the critic starts to see things from his point of view. But Obasanjo, tough old soldier that he is, has his vulnerable side. At the end of it, as he walked past, I said to him, "Good performance". "You thought so", he asked, his eyes meeting mine for approval. "Yes, you always put your case well. But I can't say I agree with it all". "I know you don't, Jonathan", and he grabbed my arm. "Come with Pierre for dinner tonight. There's so much to talk about."

There was. After such an intense day it was a relief to discuss private things: Pierre's urge to return to work in Africa and what his chances would be with various African international organizations and would Obasanjo back him. I continued my own longstanding debate with him about Christian morality and, in particular, adultery since I still felt sinful (even though I'm no longer religious) for the wrong I had done to my first wife and mother of three of my children. Obasanjo is a compassionate and incisive counsellor ……….

……….The next day we drove north to the capital of the Muslim state of Kaduna. Nigeria has a network of good arterial roads and we cover the 180 kilometres on dual carriageway rapidly, passing through an Africa which hasn't changed much in hundreds of years: simple mud houses, some tin-roofed, some thatched and no sign of electricity or even schools for most of the journey.

Three years later, the finance minister, Nenadi Usman, with whom I had become friends and stayed at her house, took me to her home village which was somewhere in this region. She and her husband, the local emir, kept a modern but not ostentatious, bungalow in the village, along with ponds full of nutritious catfish. She was very proud of this mini-industry she had started in the village. After showing me around her second home she and her husband drove me along the rutted roads, passed what were not much more than shacks, to the far end of the village. She then

showed me the local clinic which seemed almost bereft of medicines. She was a little embarrassed to show me this and we hurried on to something of which she was more proud. It was a women's group she had developed which now produced cottage-made clothes and cloth. It was their second anniversary. She made a speech and so did the emir and the woman leader. To my surprise I was invited to speak. They provided an interpreter and I launched into praise for the group but asked why it was they were not campaigning for a better clinic and school. I pointed out that the emir was here and so was the minister of finance. "Why has nothing been done?" I asked. "You must organize the other women in the village. You must push, push, push!" I hoped to embarrass my friends.

Afterwards Nenadi came up to me, smiling. "Jonathan, you speak so well. You should go into politics". I wondered if Nenadi, good Christian that she is, who prays every morning before work, would set some wheels in motion. On my next visit to Abuja I decided I would get her to take me again...........

.............We drive to the house of the widow of Obasanjo's vice-president from the time he was the military president. They were friends, and he was arrested at the same as Obasanjo. But he died in prison, and it is suspected — there was a court case in progress — that he was poisoned. We are there to pay our respects.

The widow tells about the recent religious riots. 2,000 were killed in Christian/Muslim rioting nine months ago and another 300 three months ago. "I didn't know where these riots came from. Kaduna has been a peaceful town. Christians and Muslims have lived side by side for decades. Parts of Sharia law have long been practiced in Nigeria; it has a place in the constitution. We've always had Sharia courts for Muslims — an alternative system of jurisprudence. The upset came when members of our state assembly started pushing for Sharia punishment—amputations and so on. I don't think the governor explained to the public that this wouldn't apply to Christians".

We drive along the burnt-out streets, small shops, mosques and churches, almost side by side, gutted and charred. We climb the steps up yet another ramshackle building, this time housing the Kaduna branch of Amnesty. Outside hangs a banner with the Pepsi logo affixed: "Kaduna welcomes Pierre Sane". An elderly lady walks me to the balcony. "You see those large patches of discoloured tar on the road? That's where they built bonfires and burnt people alive. I had to stand and watch it. I couldn't get out. I didn't dare go down the street."

Pierre, now dressed in full flowing Nigerian desert garb, address-es the meeting of the local Amnesty branch and a large number of NGOs. The room is crowded and everyone wants a chance to speak. Amazingly, nearly everyone is brief and to the point. I no-tice there's hardly anyone in the room over 40. But they aren't students, either. Politics in Nigeria, alas, seems to be for the old school, and NGO activity for the young, educated professionals.

"The purpose of this meeting is quite enormous", declares the chairman in the heavy cadences of Nigerian English. "People have been burnt out and don't have the wherewithal to rebuild their businesses or their homes." "The state must compensate them", says the first speaker. A leading local Muslim says, "We Nigerians are notoriously religious. Most of the time we respect each other. But a few people have abused their freedom to stir things up".

We head for the governor's office. He's a Muslim and perhaps a tolerant man—there has been no effort to erase the graffiti scrib-bled on the wall outside of his office. "Sir, sorry to say, No to Sha-ria". As with Obasanjo it's all very formal. Pierre does a succinct job of summarizing the NGOs' criticisms, and the governor an equally effective job of rebutting them. "I was glad to see that no nation, large or small, escaped criticism in your annual report—I saw it discussed on CNN".

"We are introducing a form of neighbourhood watch—drawn from various groups in each neighbourhood. We want the people to be responsible not just for security, but for maintaining the environment too. He goes through Pierre's checklist: compensation—no but assistance yes; arms—we are looking for them; NGOs—"They are welcome to come and see me"; Sharia—"We can't solve problems by fighting. We have to talk."

The meeting lasts only half an hour and we rush to the airport to catch the only plane of the day back to Lagos. Pierre says we mustn't miss it. Tomorrow he is going to be made an honourable Yoruba chief by the Alaafin (King) of Oyo for services to Amnesty.

The Yoruba kingdom of Oyo used to extend, in pre-British days, halfway across Nigeria. Today it's a shadow of its former glory—power and wealth passed long ago to the bourgeoisie and the army. Still, the traditional leaders retain the affection of their people, especially in the remote corners of the country where we are.

We arrive at the king's house—more old, corrugated iron than gold leaf, on the edge of the town of Oyo. There is a salute by toothless old men dressed in black, firing homemade muskets. The king and Pierre walk under a parasol embellished with the logo of the Gulf Oil Company, up to the reviewing stand. A succession of elderly men and women come to prostrate themselves before the king. A child, dressed as an African doll, dances. Pierre himself is dressed in the red robes of a chief. He kneels before the king, who puts red beads around his neck and a walking stick in his hand. The king speaks, calling him "one of the illustrious sons of Africa". Then it is Pierre's turn. A crowd of about 2,000 press close to hear. "Amnesty International has reached deep into the heart of Africa", Pierre says, "Deep beyond the politicians of Africa, deep into the people of Africa".

That is the amazing conclusion I've reached too. An organization begun 64 years ago in the mind of a Catholic, English lawyer of Jewish descent, has taken root in darkest Africa. I return to London and start a book which Penguin will publish on the history and doings of Amnesty. I'm inspired................

70

……………..I shared another plane journey with Obasanjo in 1999, just after he had been elected to his first term. On that occasion he threatened to throw me out at 32,000 feet. He wasn't smiling. His look was grim. Fortunately, I've known him for a long time and knew that beneath the gruff exterior he was joking. Still, I'm never quite sure if we are truly buddies, even though we can talk about almost anything. I am a journalist. He is a politician trying to build consensus in a bitterly fragmented country where corruption, poverty and criminality seethe in great urban agglomerations. This is still a country where ethnic or religious differences can turn a minor quarrel in the marketplace about ownership of a palm nut tree into an all-out pogrom, requiring the poorly trained army to impose order in its ham-fisted, sometimes brutal way.

When it comes to the army the former general feels he must defend it. Many of the senior thuggish officers who served under Abachi have been removed. Still, roll Obasanjo a question, as I did on the flight, about the army's propensity to rape and loot, the reply came back, "Tell me any commander who can stop his men raping after victory arrives when they've been two years in a hole in the ground". I said, "But you haven't been at war for years but this is still the complaint". Perhaps I shouldn't have been surprised, knowing his temper as well as I do, that he wanted to throw me out of the plane.

Well, here are in Liberia. The plane has landed. Unbelievably for a country wracked by 23 years of intermittent war, there is still a red carpet to be rolled out. It's 30 years since I've been in this godforsaken country. I was covering one of Africa's many wars — on that occasion in neighbouring Guinea — for the New York Times. Even then, slumbering peacefully under the relaxed if autocratic rule of liberated American slaves, Liberia was a third-rate place compared with the British and French ex colonies next door.

On this visit I could see that conditions had deteriorated beyond measure. Even the UN's special representative talked about filling his bath with buckets of water and eating by candlelight. How much worse it must be for those lining the road as we drove into town. The power and telephone lines were down. Until the peace agreement negotiated by Obasanjo six months before the garbage had been piled high, the markets were empty, the water supply was a trickle and cholera was rampant in the slums.

Today I could see it looked better. The markets were open, rubbish was being collected, Red Cross Land Rovers transported staff who were fighting the cholera epidemic and bringing in food and medicine. Charles Taylor, the ruthless warlord who was eventually outmanoeuvred by Obasanjo, is languishing in a luxurious government guesthouse in Calabar on the Nigerian coast. The peace deal which spirited him away on the same jet in which we arrived was secured by Obasanjo — a quid pro quo for abandoning Liberian politics and also the politics and wars of Sierra Leone and Ivory Coast in which he was the chief gunrunner, diamond smuggler and stirrer up of mayhem. (Later, Obasanjo sent him to the International Criminal Court in The Hague.)

The highlight of the trip for me was listening to Obasanjo's speech in the great hall in Government House before the (not the) good and the great of Liberia. "You must love each other. You must put the past behind you and forgive and work together to rebuild your country". I was moved, as was the American ambassador sitting beside me. Who else could address this throng, many of whom were cold-bloodied killers, and say this?

The person sitting across from me was a tall youngish man. He asked me what I did and I told him. He said he was George Weah, a footballer and had read the Herald Tribune when he'd played in Milan and Madrid. Football is not my thing. I didn't register his name. Much later I learnt who he was — he had been chosen as World Footballer of The Year. He was to become president after a free and fair election. The first thing he did was to go back to the slum in which he grew up and play in a football match of local boys.

Back in Abuja after our one-day visit to Liberia the country is losing oil revenue and once again living up to its international reputation for ethnic conflict. I am eavesdropping on a dinner conversation between Obasanjo and an ex foreign minister. It is clear that the president is preoccupied with the continuous violence in the oil town of Warri. The previous week he had told a delegation of women "that the overdependence on oil as the government's main revenue" was one of the factors for this crisis. "Oil and gas have blinded us. Oil and gas have taken us away from the values that we used to know. Oil and gas have brutalized us. We are no longer our brothers' keepers".

Five years after Obasanjo came to power the state clung too tenaciously to its omnipotent, omnipresent role. According to a Financial Times report a startling 82% of state expenditure went on funding the machinery of government.

And some has gone on grandiose projects. Abuja had seen the construction in rapid time of a world-class football stadium, sports complex and a light rail to the suburbs where the poor live and then on to the airport.

Obasanjo gets worked up when I take him to task on his priorities and suggest that with the money spent on the stadium he could have given every village clean water. "Do you know what it would cost to install clean water just in the homes of Abeokuta?" he asks, referring to his medium-sized town where he grew up. I found out he was right—the cost would be prohibitive. I think a little more—Why shouldn't Nigeria have a world class stadium when football is such a big thing and teams from all over Africa and Europe come to play, bringing in football fans from far and wide? Many have said when France won the World Cup in 2018 that it was Africa that won—most of the French squad were of African descent. Moreover, during his presidency the number of wells dug had tripled from the previous rate. Social services improved across the board.

Nigeria is no longer a simple, village-based African country. Its space engineers have worked on a British satellite launched by a Russian rocket. The head of a major Western bank, First Boston, is Nigerian. Also one has become the leader of the UK Conservative

Party. The list is a long one. As for novelists, every year brings a new writer to the fore, all walking in the footsteps of Chinua Achebe and the Nobel Prize winner, Wole Soyinka.

No one in Nigeria—and very few in Britain or America for that matter—can write more evocatively than the Nigerian author, Ben Okri. But he no longer gets it quite right; or perhaps Nigeria has indeed changed very much since the civil war period in which he set his 1991 Booker Prize-winning novel, "The Famished Road":

"Everywhere there was the crudity of wounds, the stark huts, the rusty zinc abodes, and the rubbish in the streets, children in rags and the little girls naked on the sand playing with crushed tin-cans. The sun bared the reality of our lives and everything was so harsh it was a mystery that we could understand and care for one another or anything at all."...

...The air is hot in the busy market town of Awka in the far back-yard of Nigeria. So is the talk, as happens at election time. Obasanjo and his chosen would-be successor, Umaru Yar'Adua, are on a podium, surrounded by banner-waving enthusiasts. The crowd has been bussed in by local churches even though Yar'Adua is a devout Muslim from one of the ruling families in the north.

We're in the heartland of old Biafra, the province of the mainly Christian Igbo who in the 1960s tried to break away from Nigeria. (Read the superb novel, "Half a Yellow Sun", by Chimamanda Ngozi Adichie for a bitter depiction of the war.) The Nigerian general who secured the Biafran capitulation after a bloody long-drawn-out defeat was Obasanjo. Now, given what he has learned about life, Obasanjo confided to me that he wished he would have tried to end the Biafran secession without violence, just as he accepted the ruling of the International Court of Justice on the disputed oil-rich peninsula of Bakassi, giving it to Cameroon rather than fighting for it, as popular opinion and his defence minister wanted him to.

Biafra seemed quite prosperous, although Awka is richer and less violent than other cities in the region, like Onitsha or Enugu — the southeast still has the reputation for being the roughest and most corrupt corner of the country, apart from the north where Boko Haram, a fanatical Islamic militant group, are sewing mayhem.

Driving into Awka we pass the rather grand Deeper Life Bible Church, the German Language Centre, dozens of cybercafés and the local synagogue — testament to the open nature of Nigeria's development. We also pass row upon row of well-built two-storey houses. Electric pylons dot the landscape and petrol stations without queues are on every corner.

Yar'Adua, Obasanjo's chosen presidential candidate, steps forward to address the crowd in the manner of a university lecture he once was (in chemistry) "By 2020 I want to see Nigeria as the world's twentieth industrial state. With the foundations we have dug over the last eight years there's no reason we can't do it", he says.

He won Obasanjo's respect because he was one of the few governors relatively untarnished by corruption. (Mind you, Obasanjo's judgement was not always right: the governor of Bayelsas state, Goodluck Jonathan, whom he chose as the contender for the vice-presidency and who inherited the presidency after Yar'Adua's premature death from kidney failure allowed and participated in mammoth corruption.)

Unlike Obasanjo who likes to dress up in sweeping robes, Yar'Adua wore a simple blue smock and sandals. He lacks the charisma and worldliness of his mentor, but he was thoughtful and straightforward in what he said to me. "All religions are corrupted", he tells me in his modest hotel room during a long, relaxed interview, "but all religions are about love, kindness, justice and tolerance. These virtues are difficult for governments to put into practice. And this is what I've tried to do in my state."

When Obasanjo became president in 1999 many of the state governors in Nigeria's Muslim north tried to embarrass him by imposing Sharia law, which mandates severe bodily punishments like chopping off a limb or decapitation. Yar'Adua resisted this, he told me, at least in its strictest form. I asked him about a young woman who was plastered across the headlines who was convicted of adultery and was supposed to be severely punished. "Look, he said, "the Koran says you have to have four witnesses of an act of adultery. How is that possible? She should not have been arrested and tried. If the high court does not overturn the conviction, I will pardon her".

When I asked him how he planned to deal with the violence in the oil-producing Niger delta — one of the country's running sores — he replies. "By patient negotiation", adding, with a laugh, "You know Obasanjo, with his military manner, is not very good at patience." In fact, not long after he won the election he succeeded in fashioning in careful negotiations (his main negotiator was vice-president Goodluck Jonathan) a peace deal with the militants which gave the country thirteen years of peace until 2015, when violence, oil sabotage and oil theft started up again.

Down in the delta, I found contradictions wherever I turned. Most political and human rights activists here pursue their causes non-violently. But the military are still strong. One of the problems over the years is that the big western oil companies attempted to buy off the most ferocious militants, who simply pocketed what was offered and then a few months later demanded more.

In the mangrove swamps, after I'd hired a boat from young men lounging by the river, smoking weed, I saw rich, highly productive oil wells cheek by jowl with fishermen's villages made of reeds and grass, so frail they look as if the next big wind would blow them away. Yet in Port Harcourt, the oil capital and up to now one of the most miserable towns in Nigeria, building work is booming, primary and secondary school enrolment is increasing and drinking water supplies are spreading. The governor of Rivers state, Peter Odili, boasted to me about new roads and new small businesses, even as he proudly showed me around the Saddam-Hussein-type palace he had built for himself.

Back in Abuja I asked Obasanjo if it was God or the devil who gave Nigeria oil. "God", he replies. "But the devil is manipulating it." He went on to explain that although he feels that nowadays the oil money is being used more productively, Nigeria would have developed more harmoniously without it. "Our non-oil sectors, agriculture in particular, are growing at 8% a year. If we had no oil we would be going just as fast, without all the trouble oil brings." One astonishing example of this growing diversity is the fact that "Nollywood", the country's burgeoning film industry, has now overtaken both Hollywood and Bollywood in the number of films produced each year, and employs one million people, making it the second largest source of jobs after agriculture.

The World Values Survey found that year that Nigerians are the happiest people in the world. Why Nigeria? I visited an up-country village, near the confluence of the Niger and Benue rivers. Everyone I passed in the village of 5000 people said "hello" to me, often with a smile, and yet I knew many of them had barely enough to eat. I was given lunch by the headmaster of the local technical school, Peter Ikani, cooked over a wood fire outside by his 28-year old daughter, Eli. It was simple but deliciously spicy goat stew served with yams. Peter apologized for receiving me in his "hovel" (which it nearly was) and explained that teachers are badly paid and often enough paid late. Peter reads books and is thoughtful and religious. Eli is able and articulate but, unable to afford university, has a low-level job in Abuja, a five-hour bus journey away. Yes, they both say earnestly, Nigerians are happy people. It has nothing to do with the politicians, good or bad. Peter puts it down to God and music: "We have great religious faith. Whether Christians in the south or Muslims in the north, we all believe ardently that God is looking after us". Eli adds, perhaps with greater realism: "I can take you to people in the village who are hungry, who are not happy, and God is just in their lives as a solace. One reason why many of us are happy is that we don't ask too much."

A few days earlier I had dined in Abuja with Princess Gloria, the daughter of an Igbo king and appointments secretary to the president. She explained it this way: "We feel full of music and love of God. And it's the amount of love we get when we are children. We are smothered in love from parents, aunts, cousins and grand-parents". An engineer who was dining with us added: "It was in our old tribal traditions and religion built on that. Have you ever seen such a religious people? Look at all the new mosques and churches. Of course, it can go too far and we become too fatal-istic".

At a newspaper editors' forum where I had been invited to speak, the previous speaker, a freedom of information advocate said, "I read about the survey. I was surprised and not surprised. If you look at our problems, it is unimaginable to say we are happy. But then Nigerians appear to have very thick skins. Fela Kui, the leg-endary singer of the 1970s had a song, "Shuffering and shmiling".

On my last day on this visit — I have been to Nigeria at least a doz-en times — I attended church with Obasanjo. He had a chapel in the presidential grounds and loved to lead the singing and give one of the sermons. "I'm happy", he told the congregation, "but the only time I had real joy in my life (this is a man who has had nine wives and 20 children) was when I was in prison. Then there was just God and my fellow prisoners, whom I had to help".

As I said before, I call Obasanjo a friend, so perhaps you want to discount some of what I now write. He has been the most success-ful president Nigeria has ever had, both in what he has accom-plished at home with his imaginative economic policies, and abroad, where, as in Liberia, he has waded into difficult situations and helped put a country back on its feet.

I have seen Nigeria under his watch move from being stuck in the ditch transformed to a country with a growth rate of 7% a year — nearly as good as China and India. I have seen the Nigerians en-joying — and taking care of their freedoms — free speech, protest, newspapers, TV and the independent power and confidence of Congress and the courts.

Such was his achievement that I watch Nigeria in pain these days as its economy slumps. The falling oil price is one reason. Another is the frittering away by the Jonathan government of the sovereign fund Obasanjo had built up to use on a rainy day. Corruption, aided by Jonathan, is another. Jonathan's two successors have been almost as bad.

If Nigeria could once again hit the sort of stride that it achieved under Obasanjo then not only Nigeria but all Africa would be lifted many notches higher. If it fails nearly the entire continent will feel the effects. I will go there again soon for more "talk, talk, talk" with Olusegun Obasanjo and to examine what remains of his legacy.

Chapter 5
My life-long comrade, Valeria the nun, and her friends, Lula and the Cardinal, and big change in Brazil

"Antônio das Mortes," a film by Glauber Rocha, tells the story of a small village in northeast Brazil. A group of land-hungry peasants have taken to banditry. The local landowner and police chief decide they need Antônio das Mortes, a professional assassin. Antônio arrives and meets the peasants' leader in the village square.

Soon the peasant is dead, a knife through his heart. The peasants weep and dance. Antônio is overcome. He asks the landlord to open the granary and help the near-starving people. The landlord refuses. In a vision, Antônio sees the peasant leader crucified on a gnarled tree. A virgin appears and asks Antônio to seek revenge. He is persuaded and, with the help of the police chief's drunken assistant, takes on the landowner's private army and destroys it.

Fact or fiction? A bit of both. Antônio das Mortes did exist, and so did the Cangaceiros, the bandits, and their leader, Lampião. In the mid-1930s these rebel peasants, with their wide-brim hats studded with bright metals, were wiped out. In the late 1950s they were replaced by the more sophisticated Ligas Camponesas (peasant leagues), organised by a Marxist lawyer from Recife, Francisco Julião. The Ligas occupied land and threatened landlords who did not redistribute it. They too were violently suppressed. Today Brazilians recall the time of the Cangaceiros as Americans recall the days of cowboys and Indians.

Visiting Pilõezinhos—a village of just over a thousand families of mixed Indian and European descent in the northeast, 120 miles from the city of Recife—it is difficult to believe that Antônio's story is the local living history. Around the quiet, orderly village square are the houses of richer peasants built in a simple Portuguese colonial style with yellow or blue façades and roofs of red clay tiles. Rising uphill into the mists are the orange groves and the sugar plantations of the latifundiario, the absentee landowners of European descent who, from faraway Recife or even Rio, still give the orders and take most of the money. At first sight the lush, haunting beauty of Pilõezinhos makes it look like the kind of place a Gauguin might make famous. A closer look reveals a Picasso mask.

It is hard for a long-standing observer of Brazil to imagine that the future of its charismatic president, Luiz Inácio Lula da Silva, or Lula, who grew up in another impoverished village in the northeast, will be decided by villagers like those of Pilõezinhos. Until the 1990s, Brazil's elites did not much care what these people thought. That has changed.

Twenty-five years ago it is dusk here in Pilõezinhos. Coloured lights decorate the square. From my hammock in one of the small houses I can see the church silhouetted in the gloom. It is the night of São João, St John the Baptist, one of the biggest feasts in the Brazilian calendar. The men have been out in the heavy rain bringing in wood to build small bonfires in front of their houses. The wood has been drenched by weeks of winter downpours, but the penalty for not lighting a fire is said to be death before the next São João.

The music and dancing that I am expecting do not materialise. Most of the young men are away in Recife, working on construction sites. Those who remain — women, children and older men — struggle to eke out an existence in the shadow of a feudal land-ownership system that has hardly changed in four centuries. It is not a time for dancing.

Back then, a child in Pilõezinhos died from undernourishment or illness every day. The undertaker lived in Guarabira, a market town three miles away along a potholed road. There were stacks of plywood children's coffins in his shopfront, painted blue with white crosses on top. A father often only heard of the death of his child when he returned home from his job elsewhere, three or four times a year.

Dom Marcelo, the local Catholic bishop, also lived in Guarabira. He slept on an old door supported on bricks. Forty-nine years old, dressed in slacks and an open shirt, he accused the economic system of driving the people to destitution. "Things have always been bad here," he explained to me. "Now they are getting worse. Since the commercial farmers came in the last few years, buying out the feudal owners and putting land down to sugar cane or cattle ranching, tens of thousands of families have been evicted. You have only to go to the market to see them." In 1969 Marcelo had been jailed for two months, falsely accused of being part of Carlos Marighella's guerrilla movement, which was attempting to overthrow the military dictatorship.

Pilõezinhos was depressed then, but to see the real abomination of 1970s Brazil, a visitor to the northeast had to go to Recife. A quarter of the city's 2m people were living in its favelas (shanty towns), where half of the houses lacked sanitation. It seemed then — and many millions of Brazilians still live in slums like this — that in Recife, if disease didn't get you, the criminals would.

Two years earlier, in 1976, I had flown into Recife to meet its notorious archbishop, Helder Camara, whom Time magazine called the "red bishop." The regime had banned Camara from the Brazilian media, but his pastoral work continued. He put me up in a 17th-century convent by the sea. At breakfast the morning after I arrived, a striking young woman walked in, dressed in jeans and a t-shirt. "Meet my favourite nun," the red archbishop said, and since that day Valéria Rezende and I have been friends. It was she who introduced me to Piloezinhos.

I first met Camara when he came to London to speak to a conference of pro Third World activists, the Haslemere Group, of which I was one of the organizers. "The world will change", he told us, "when the small people start to believe in the other small people".

He invited me to stay with him in Brazil. To my surprise I found this diminutive man dressed in black waiting for me at the airport. Here, I thought, is a very brave man. One of his closest associates, a priest, had been recently murdered. His house, a small three-room affair tacked onto the back of a church, was machine-gunned three times. Later I asked Valeria why she considered him so significant. "He can talk to anyone", she answered. "The beggars who come to his door talk to him for two hours over breakfast. If he gets in a taxi he will talk to the driver the entire journey. The most important thing about him is not what he does, but what he gets others to do. He has a gift for helping people to discover they can do great things".

Camara has been one of those who pushed the church—including the Cardinal of Sao Paulo—to stand up against the government. The cardinal may be untouchable but not bishops and priests. A gang of self-proclaimed "anti-communists" kidnapped a bishop, stripped him, painted his body with red dye and dumped him in an alley way. The same year another bishop went to a police station with a priest to investigate the torture of two women prisoners. After a sharp argument, a policeman shot the priest to death before the bishop's eyes.

Nevertheless, the military government had to tolerate the Church. An overwhelming majority of Brazilians are Catholics even if only in name. In every favela there is a priest, a nun or lay worker, not just comforting the sick and distributing the sacraments, but helping to organize the inhabitants to win from the municipal government drinking water, sanitation and the right to tenure. The military regime knows any attack on the church would inflame passions and make it an outcast in many parts of the world. In both Brazil and Chile the Church used its muscle to resist the military. In Argentina it did not. The present pope, Francis, the ex-archbishop of Buenos Aires, was one of those who, for the most part, kept his powder dry. During the difficult years of repression from 1968 to 1976 it was the Brazilian church that looked for "lost persons" who mysteriously disappeared, and that kept track of those who were jailed and made constant representation on their behalf. "All these activities", Valeria explained to me, "are like a multitude of termites all eating away at the military regime." At some point, she said, the effect would coalesce. "The small individual nibbles of these termites, repeated a hundred fold, a thousand fold will eventually undermine and transform the infrastructure of the government from beneath".

Camara and I, over many years, spent hours talking about revolution, rights and morality. He was insistent that violence must never be used in retaliation. It is a political tool he abhorred. "Revolutionary violence is too often paternalistic" he once told me, "imposing ideas on people that they are not ready for". He preferred the slow way of educating, cajoling, pushing, "using weapons that armies cannot use".

"As for peace, it's well known that there can be instances of false peace, with the same deceptive beauty as stagnant marches in moonlight. The peace which speaks to us, which moves us, for which we are prepared to give our lives, presupposes that the rights of all are fully respected: the rights of God and the rights of man".

As a student, Valéria had also been accused of working for Carlos Marighella. Her boyfriend, Betto, ran guns. They were both captured. With her air of feminine innocence, she talked her way out of it, but Betto went to jail for four years. Years later, their romance long broken up, they met at a party to celebrate Betto's release and were dancing samba together. "What are your plans?" asked Betto. "I have decided to become a nun," Valéria replied. "That's interesting," said Betto. "I have decided to become a monk." The Church, both of them felt, offered the last remaining opportunity to change their country; it was the only institution with a modicum of independence and idealism. For many decades Valéria worked with the youth of rural outposts like Pilõezinhos, although, like Betto, she later became a well-known novelist as well. A few years ago she won Brazil's top literature prize. (In fact she won it twice.) When I first knew her and for decades after she never talked about being a novelist but after she was 50 the desire emerged and now it has her in its grip.

Valeria has been one of the most special of all my friends. I recall when she visited London and we were walking through Soho and past a porn cinema she asked me if I would take her to a film. I never did, only because she ran out of time. Once in Sao Paulo we were having dinner in an open-air restaurant. I leant across the table and kissed her and she responded. Later I took her home and near the convent's doors we daringly smooched. The next morning she came to my room in the hotel to pick me up. Neither of us mentioned the night before and never have ever since. Maybe it's gone into one of her novels, but as I don't read Portuguese I don't know.

Whenever I arrived from England she would meet me at the airport and the first thing we did after we got in a taxi was to go into a shack at the road side and buy a bottle of cane juice and orange juice to dilute the 40% spirit. Soon we were pretty tipsy and held each other's hand. At the weekend she would take me down to see the American priests who lived in a favela. On Saturday they and some other nuns would go down to a little house the diocese owned and talk and drink beer or cane juice. But I never saw any hint of suppressed romance!

Later she decided to spend a quiet year alone in a little house in Piloezinhos. After years of arduous work in the outback and riding to off-beat towns and villages on all-night decrepit buses she told me she needed some peace. I stayed with Bishop Marcello but every morning after breakfast I would take the local bus on the rutted road to visit Valeria. I would spend all day there and apart from the occasional walk I spent my time in her hammock or helped her cook. We spent most of the day either reading, talking and listening to classical music on her small, cheap, tape recorder. (For once I could concentrate on each note and we had marvellous discussions about each piece.) I stayed 4 days and the time passed too quickly. I learnt so much from her. She was and is able to see into the heart of the politics of Brazil. She also spoke with profundity on region, belief and philosophy. She is a very religious woman attached to her order of nuns—today she uses her book income to subsidize the retired nuns in her order. But she would miss Sunday mass and not be bothered. I never saw her pray. She told me, "My work is my prayer."

On the night of the feast of São João Valeria and I talked about the absence of music. "Next year," she said, "we'll help the peasants get it going again. They are so beaten down that they don't have any value left in their traditions." As we talked, the villagers began moving along the dark road carrying a statue of the saint, each with a candle. Behind them in the darkness the plantations stretched for miles.

In 1980, a few years after our first encounter, Valéria, using Betto's connections, took me to meet Lula—Ignacio da Silva, the man who much later was to become the Workers' Party first president of Brazil. He was then the radical leader of the São Paulo car workers' union, a 34-year-old lathe operator who had just been in prison for calling a strike. Police had attacked the strikers, and one of Lula's comrades, a member of a Catholic workers' movement, had been killed. At the funeral, half a dozen bishops and 200 priests walked through the centre of São Paulo. Paulo Evaristo Arns, cardinal of the world's largest diocese, walked with them and said the funeral mass. The military president, General João Baptista Figueiredo, accused Arns of inciting the workers. On the way to see Lula I visited the cardinal, who had just been told by the government that the Church's small "base communities"—organisations found in every favela and thousands of villages—were the same as communist cells.

Communist fellow travellers or not, without the support of Arns, Camara and much of the rest of the church so many years ago, Lula would not have become what he is today, the dominant figure in Brazilian politics. Lula himself has never been religious. "I'm not inspired by great themes, great philosophers," he told me then in a small but comfortable house near his factory, "I'm led by my own experience: 20 years on the shop floor, a life of hunger in the northeast, a mother who had to work 12 hours a day to feed eight children, crossing the country in a truck to find a job."

What brought Lula and the cardinal together was not just a common concern for the poor, but a conviction that the military regime could be undermined without violence. Lula, the cardinal told me with appreciation, had even abolished picket lines from his union's strikes. I spoke to Lula when his reputation as a firebrand was probably at its peak, yet he went out of his way to underline his moderate approach, a line he has kept to over the years since. "I believe that the government is much more frightened by the seriousness of our proposals for the transformation of society than by the crazy propositions of the lefties," he told me. "The working class has begun to discover itself, and it is finding its identity without doing anything silly... It is better to go forward just one millimetre but knowing we won't have to go two millimetres backward later." As if to underline his caution, he added, "We can only improve our situation if we don't impose our thoughts. I don't propose what is on my mind. I propose what I get from the hearts of the workers."

For an outsider visiting a still turbulent Latin America at a time when Che Guevara had been in his Bolivian grave for only 13 years, the striking thing was that despite Brazil's economic and political ferment, the extreme left was marginal. The debate was between the military right, with its technocrats and middle and upper-class supporters, and what might be called the "radical moderates," in the form of the Church and Lula's incipient Workers' party.

Cardinal Arns, however, was careful in my company not to endorse the Workers' party, and he completely rejected the parallel I drew between Brazil, with its political prelates, and Iran, where a movement led by a mullah, Ayatollah Khomeini, had recently overthrown the shah. "Brazil has produced two or three Khomeinis in the past," the cardinal told me. "But there's no one in the church today who has a vocation for that. I have no desire to grow a beard or take power."

The radical moderates did eventually take power in Brazil, through the ballot box, after the generals had voluntarily given way to a civilian regime that later called elections in 1985. Following three unsuccessful tries, in 1989, 1994 and 1998, Lula finally won the presidency in October 2002. He became Brazil's most popular ever president.

The year now is 2005 and I am back in Pilõezinhos. It is 17 years since I last spent time in the village. Valéria, who no longer lives there, is with me. Much seems as I left it. The village still rests in the green hills, its yellow colonial church has the same blue doors, its square is still crisscrossed with the traffic of mules carrying sugar cane and pineapples. The gushing flood-filled river still races between the breadfruit plantations.

But as my eyes focused through the heat haze, I started to see the differences. The square had half a dozen cars parked around it, and a batch of motorcycle taxis that can spin a passenger to Guarabira in five minutes on a new metaled road. There were a couple of supermarkets with far more goods than the beans, rice, pots and pans that used to be sold in the dark little shops. There was a post office, a hardware shop doubling as a bank branch, two dispensaries selling generic medicines and an agricultural adviser marketing advice and modern seeds to the peasants.

Walking around the village, looking up old acquaintances, I learnt that less visible changes have also taken place. Land reform means many people now have their own land for the first time in their lives. The peasants earn more, and rural workers over 65 now receive the entire monthly minimum wage as a pension. Lula's most important and popular social innovation has been the Bolsa Família—built on a more elementary scheme begun by his predecessor—which pays families 64 reals (£16, $20) a month (a significant if modest sum) on the condition that their children attend school.

Fatima Trajano, a graduate of one of Valéria's "base communities" from the old days and now deputy mayor, took me to the village health and dental centre. The doctor told me that children are no

89

longer dying, and that the birth rate is falling; 40 per cent of couples are using contraception, which is free. We walked down the street from the clinic to a primary school bursting with happy faces. In one classroom the geography books were open at "Europe," about which the children have just written short essays. It reminded me of a previous visit in 1988, when I was out walking with Valéria and a peasant asked her what I was talking. It was the first time he had ever heard a foreign language. Now the class listened as I spoke slowly in Spanish, which they seem to understand, and three quarters of them quickly raised their hands when I asked them what the capital of my country was.

Fatima invited me into her simple, neat house with its running water and two flush toilets. Half the village now has these facilities, she said. I remember the old days with a shudder: the dark, dank shed in Valéria's garden and the toad as large as my two hands together, keeping vigil over the dry toilet. After lunch of local fish, beans, rice and fruit, Fatima took me to see another innovation: a town hall in a converted shop front, with a square of tables for the elected councillors and six rows of chairs for those who want to see how local democracy works.

Thirty-five years ago, Pilõezinhos seemed to be still sleepwalking, struck down by poverty and hopelessness. Today its streets were busy with bustling adults and skipping children. The religious festivals, I'm told, are celebrated in full swing. "So all this happened before Lula became president?" I ask Valéria.

"Yes, but Lula has been on the scene and pushing this country hard for over 40 years," she replies. "And don't forget what the Church has done with its base communities. We got the people in villages like this all over the northeast to take their destiny into their own hands. They pushed on one side, Lula and his Workers' party pushed on another, and the country has moved and is now going to move faster."

Leaving Pilõezinhos on its smart new road, wondering if I will ever go back, I sensed again a feeling that I get nowhere else in the world. For all Brazil's appalling inequalities, its history of military rule, its favelas that may be the most violent slums on earth, its long subjugation of black and Indian people — it remains somehow the archetypal relaxed, tolerant and gregarious society. Copacabana beach, the carnival, the samba, the hospitality, the sexual freedom: these are not just concoctions of the tourist brochure.

Brazil is richly blessed. It is home to the world's largest tropical forest and has the world's largest reservoirs of fresh water. It is self-sufficient in oil and has a wealth of hydroelectric power. It is the world's fifth largest country, both in population (215m) and in size. It is now highly industrialized. Over 80 per cent of the population is urbanized. The economy of São Paulo city is larger than that of Argentina. Few countries offer such geographic variety and natural wealth, but for the best part of four centuries too much has been squandered: the Amazon raped, the poor exploited, institutions abused. The mismanagement has gone on so long that to many it seems endemic.

Despite all this, Brazil has had periods of sustained growth. Indeed, according to the economic historian, Angus Maddison, for the first 80 years of the 20th century it was, along with Taiwan, the fastest-growing economy in the world. Even today, after many setbacks, it is the world's ninth largest economy. Its average gross national income per capita is $3,000. This compares with China's $1,500 and India's $620. Can Brazil now make the final leap into the ranks of developed countries? Can it rediscover the recipe for fast economic growth, but this time a growth that lifts all boats? Can it reduce its huge gap between rich and poor, which the World Bank argues is holding back the pace of economic growth? Brazil is still the most unequal country in Latin America, and Latin America the most unequal region in the world.

Lula's predecessor, the centrist president Fernando Henrique Cardoso, had laid many of the foundations for progress in his two terms in office (1995-2003). Under Cardoso, Brazil achieved fiscal discipline and social reform for the first time ever, with a stable currency, a rapid increase in primary education and large-scale land redistribution. But even with a big congressional majority,

Cardoso was stymied on many important issues. His second term attempted to slim the bureaucracy, reform the judiciary and reduce the tax concessions of the rich. They were all thwarted. His popularity shrank.

Denied a majority, Lula's government was cursed with the necessities of coalition horse-trading—although the Workers' Party formed the biggest group in the Chamber of Deputies and shared third place in the Senate, the upper house, it couldn't govern alone. The special interests empowered by the situation comprised a broad mix: the judiciary, the still powerful Latifundia, an inept and often brutal police force, public sector workers with their 100 per cent state pensions, and the well-to-do students who received a disproportionate share of state handouts.

Administration, as everyone knows, is not the former lathe operator's strength. Three financial scandals while he was president took their toll on Lula's reputation, one involving illegal contributions to his Workers' party, another vote-buying in congress and accusations from Sao Paulo's chief prosecutor that Lula solicited illegal contributions to his party from business and oil companies. Lula claims he knew nothing about this and that the main culprit was José Dirceu, his chief of staff. After the second scandal he sacked Dirceu. Later, out of power, he was imprisoned after a rather ridiculous charge that he received a beach front flat in return for authorising some contracts. He denied it. In fact, the beach is not pretty and the nearby town uninspiring. If he were corrupt he'd have chosen a better place than this.

Lula's then new chief of staff, Dilma Rousseff, who later became Brazil's first woman president, told me in her office next to Lula's: "It is more difficult to make this economy not grow than to make it grow. Our exports are growing faster than China's, as China and India continue to suck in Brazil's soya beans, meat, mineral products and aircraft". I had brought her copies of articles I had written earlier about Lula. She read them and then said I knew more than Brazilian journalists. Of course, I was flattered.

In terms of income distribution, Lula's government built only modestly on Cardoso's achievements. In a 2004 World Bank study, Vinod Thomas, the former head of the bank's mission in Brasilia, estimated that up to 20 per cent of Brazil's people could be classed as poor, compared with 16 per cent in China and 35 per cent in India. The very poor — earning less than $1 a day — were about 8 to 13 percent of the population. (By the end of Lula's term of office it was down to 3% according to the Economist.) David de Ferranti, until recently vice-president for Latin America of the World Bank, writes, "Brazil is not a poor country. The 'poverty gap' [the amount that would be required in direct income support to raise all the poor over the poverty threshold] is only 3.4 percent of national income. Brazil spends much, much more than this on various forms of public outlays, much of which benefits the middle class".

Nevertheless, since Cardoso's reforms, poverty has been steadily falling, income distribution improving, especially among younger people, and equality of opportunity widening. Brazil has reduced its infant mortality faster than most developing countries — decreasing by half between 2000 and 2020. Its primary school enrollment has increased quickly. But for the workforce to compete with China and India, the schools need better paid teachers and an increase in secondary school attendance (currently less than 40 per cent), and the universities have to widen their intake. In 2004, the World Bank claimed South Africa had made better progress than Brazil in closing the education gap between whites and non-whites.

Land reform remains a cry, but the issue has lost its radical appeal. Under Cardoso, 600,000 families were settled on redistributed land. The process has continued slowly under Lula, but the promised agricultural revolution has not materialised, and the first two years of Lula's government saw a wave of protests and illegal property invasions by the Landless Workers' Movement, the descendants of the Cangaceiros and the Ligas Camponesas. Land redistribution protesters appeared to go quiet, partly because of the country's relatively upbeat mood, and partly because of their income from Bolsa Familia.

In the favelas of Recife, the mood was more hopeful than I had ever seen it. Many of the old slums have been improved and upgraded into fairly respectable dwellings, complete with bathrooms. There are similar improvements in São Paulo, where the favelas' main streets now boast massive supermarkets selling the goods of the global consumer society. Most of the country's slums, however, including those of Recife and São Paulo, remain havens of crime, much of it drug driven. The crime and murder rate in São Paulo, although falling, is the highest for any urban agglomeration in the world. In mid-2004 Lula had to send the army into the favelas of Rio de Janeiro. In Brazil, according to a report in the Economist, the number of deaths per capita by shooting is far higher than in the US or South Africa. Little has been done to reform the police forces, which in Brazil's highly devolved federal structure are the responsibility of state governors and local mayors, and thus effectively beyond the reach of Lula's Administration. However later in his term the situation became so bad that Lula and then Rousseff sent the army into some of the favelas.

It is always dangerous to underestimate the pull of Lula. The former union leader has a deep hold on the affections not just of the inhabitants of the favelas and of Brazil's many Pilõezinhos, but also of liberal middle-class Brazilians (albeit rather less than before) who have dreamt for decades of a fairer Brazil. When Lula speaks at a rally or on television, the audience is gripped. He has dominated Brazilian politics for a good part of a century. Win or lose, he will continue to do so for a while yet. In 2023 he won the presidency once again. He singled out land reform as being prominent on his agenda.

Chapter 6
Guatemala —
No political prisoners,
only political murders

In Guatemala there has been no paramount leader[1] in the struggle for human rights and democracy to single out. Indeed, there is
no defining moment when one could say that things started to get
better after a particular event. Guatemala is simply one of the contemporary world's worst horror stories that gradually, often
enough imperceptibly, got better but with still a long way to go.
Amnesty was in at the struggle from the beginning. Some of its
exposés gained world attention, but none profoundly changed the
situation for the better. Improvement came by the dripping of
water on hard stone, incrementally, painfully slowly but over time
clearly ameliorating an appalling state of affairs, where not that
long ago assassinations and disappearances were as common and
as prevalent as cars and motorbikes on the capital's overcrowded
streets.

For me, it was a journalistic nut to crack—of the hard kind. It was
the sort of challenge I like—unveiling lies and injustice, cruelty
and cover up. I've done a few of these but Guatemala was a country that I kept coming back to. For decades now I've tried not to
take my eye off the ball.

Guatemala is part of the isthmus that links the great continents of
North and South America. In the 1970s and early 1980s it was,
along with El Salvador and Nicaragua, the part of the world

---

1   The controversial Indian leader Rigoberta Menchu came to prominence late
     on in the events I describe, although she was active from the early 1980s, but
     mainly as an exile. She became both world- and Guatemala- renowned when
     she was awarded the Nobel Peace Prize in 1993. She has been a major figure in
     creating sympathy around the world for indigenous peoples, and also for the
     guerrilla movement within Guatemala.

where human rights were most violated. Proportionally to its population, more people werc tortured and killed for their beliefs than anywhere else on the globe. For centuries, since the Spanish moved their initial interest in Central America to the vast continent to the south, these countries have been a backwater. (Costa Rica and Panama, also Central American countries, have different histories, the latter because of US occupation of the Canal Zone and the former because of its lack of feudal history and its distinct, liberal political culture.) The rest have all been feudal, reactionary states par excellence, long used to the writ of the local strong man. In the 1970s they became the focus of superpower interest. In each of these countries anti-establishment guerrilla groups were formed with discreet support from communist Cuba—but also from Venezuela, Panama, Costa Rica, Mexico, Peru, Ecuador and Bolivia and, it was said, without any evidence, from Moscow. The USA, long the passive supporter of the status quo, became increasingly an active participant, not always on the side of the dictators, but more often than not.

In 1981 I made my first visit to Guatemala, struck by an interview I had recently done with Thomas Hammarberg, who was then Amnesty's secretary-general, in which he had singled out Guatemala as Amnesty's number one priority. The organisation, I learnt, was just about to publish a report in which it concluded that the selection of targets for detention and murder, and the deployment of official forces for extra-legal operations could be pinpointed to secret offices in an annexe to Guatemala's National Palace, under the direct control of the President of the Republic.

Before I left, Hammarberg cautioned me: "Guatemala is not a typical Amnesty country — there are no political prisoners, only political killings." Amnesty's usual practice of dealing with human rights violations—the adoption of prisoners—was fruitless in the Guatemalan case, he explained. Most of the time, news of an arrest arrived after the prisoner was dead. When the notification had been immediate and Amnesty had been able to intervene within hours of the arrest, there had been a handful of successes. But, he added, no more than ten or 15 in the whole of the preceding ten years.

Surprisingly, to enter Guatemala was not difficult. Passport control was lax and it was easy to disappear into the airport throng with only a tourist visa. There were a few soldiers lazing in the sunshine. Even a visit to the press spokesman for the army, Major Francisco Djalma Dominguez, whose predecessor had been murdered by guerrillas a year before, was made without inspection of papers and with only a pleasant middle-aged secretary to question my purpose. The single soldier on the doorstep was daydreaming.

All this was deceptive. Guatemala, I soon found, was a country in the grip of fear. Government critics, with very rare exceptions, would not be seen talking to a foreign reporter inside Guatemala. To do so was to court assassination. Every day the morning newspapers had more of the same: ten or a dozen bodies discovered, another wave of killing. The bodies of the victims were found piled up in ravines, dumped at roadsides or buried in mass graves.

Since 1944 the Guatemalan ruling class had been living in fear of a left-wing revolution. In that year a military rebellion broke the grip of 14 years' dictatorial rule by Jorge Ubico. A university don, Juan Jose Arevalo, was given the job of sorting out the long legacy of misrule, social deprivation and economic inequality. He stepped down in 1951 and in free and fair elections his defence minister, Colonel Jacobo Arbenz Guzman, took over the reins of government.

Guatemala, at that time, was a classic "banana republic". Arbenz, a determined reformer, decided to end once and for all the United Fruit Company's control of vast estates and its near monopoly of banana production. The first beneficiaries were to be the Indian population. Despite the spectacular cultural heritage of the native Indians — their direct ancestors, the Mayans, built mammoth temples and houses and pioneered major breakthroughs in astronomy and mathematics — they were a people who had experienced worsening poverty right through the 20th century. The Indians made up half of the population, and they were becoming increasingly overcrowded on their traditional territory, the mountainside fields. Their infant mortality rate was high, their diet was deteriorating annually, and younger sons were reduced to scraping a living on precipitous slopes that barely held the soil to the mountainside.

Arbenz issued a decree expropriating parts of large estates — in the main their uncultivated portions. In doing so, he took on imperial capitalism at its crudest. The United Fruit Company had for decades had its way throughout Central America, much of the Caribbean and parts of South America. By the 1950s United Fruit's investment in Guatemala accounted for almost two-thirds of the country's total foreign capital. It owned 2,500,000 square kilometres of territory and the country's single railway line, and had great influence in many of Guatemala's most important institutions.

Arbenz's experiments not only threatened United Fruit, they aroused Washington's fears. At the height of the Cold War, the US government was afraid of anything that smacked of communist influence. No matter that Arbenz himself was clearly not a communist and that only four out of 56 Guatemalan congressmen were self-confessed communists at that time. The CIA was asked by President Eisenhower to help overthrow Arbenz, using as a cover a group of mercenaries and exiles. The deed was done, United Fruit retrieved its estates, Arbenz and his sympathisers were hunted down and killed or went into hurried exile. Arbenz's successors ruled largely by decree. Occasionally there were street demonstrations led by students and trade unionists. But nothing really disturbed the status quo until 1960. Then a small group of nationalist army officers attempted an uprising. It came to nothing in itself. It was the start, however, of a guerrilla campaign which waxed and waned for most of the next 40 years.

By 1966 the guerrillas' strongholds in the mountain ranges of Sierra de Las Minas and Sierra de Santa Cruz seemed a genuine threat to the government, which, with the aid of paramilitary civilian groups, moved ruthlessly to suppress them. Colonel John Webber, the US military attaché, was reported by *Time* magazine on 26 January 1968 to have acknowledged that it was his "idea" to mobilise these groups,[2] which were the precursors of the "independent" civilian death-squads that caused mayhem until the early 21st century. In June 1966 the first leaflets of the *Mano Blanca* (White Hand) appeared. (Mano was the acronym for the *Movimiento Anti-Communista Nacional Organizado* (National Organized Anti-Communist Movement).) The guerrilla movement did not re-emerge until the mid-1970s, when a group surfaced calling itself, disarmingly, the Guerrilla Army of the Poor. By 1980 there were another three groups at work in different parts of the country, concentrated in the highlands and mountains of the north – the People's Armed Organization, the Revolutionary Armed Forces and a breakaway branch of Guatemala's communist trade union. Their members were few – the army told me that there were only 200; sympathisers were said to be one or two thousand. But they were multiplying fast and, to the surprise of observers of the Latin American scene, were winning a great deal of support and membership from the Indians. (When Che Guevara was hunted down and killed by the Bolivian army in 1967, it was widely observed by both left and right that he made the mistake of thinking the Latin American Indians and mestizos would be willing supporters of the guerrillas. In fact, they were too apathetic and fearful and he was quickly isolated. It was Guatemala that became the first country in Latin America where significant numbers of Indians were politically active to the point of lending their support in measurable terms to a guerrilla effort to overthrow the government. However, while the guerrilla movements' activities were sporadic, the right-wing pro-government death squads operated on full throttle. Amnesty International from the beginning always maintained that the association of the death-squads with important key government and political figures was close enough to cause serious con-

---

2   US government documents now made available to the public make it clear that this was official government policy.

cern. In its report of 1980 it stopped short of saying that the killings were directed by the government. Amnesty at that time was still awaiting irrefutable evidence to confirm its suspicions.

The nuanced approach was discarded on 18 February 1981. In one of the most outspoken reports ever issued by Amnesty, it stated unequivocally: "People who oppose or are imagined to oppose the government are systematically seized without warrant, tortured and murdered. These tortures and murders are part of the deliberate and long-standing programme of the Guatemalan government." The government, for its part, denied having made a single political arrest or having held a single political prisoner. The "disappearances",[3] senior government officials told me, were brought about by right-wing and left-wing death-squads. The Amnesty report is an accumulation of horrors that pointed a firm finger at the government. My own conversations with exiles in Costa Rica and with the vice-president of Guatemala, who fled the country in late 1980, backed it up.

Nearly 3,000 Guatemalans were seized without warrant and killed in the years immediately following General Lucas Garcia's accession to the presidency of Guatemala in 1978. (And thousands more subsequently.) Many of them were tortured. Death for some had been quick and clean, a bullet in the head. Others had died slowly and painfully, suffocated in a rubber hood or strangled with a garrotte. One letter received by Amnesty International described a secret grave in a gorge, used by army units who had seized and murdered the leaders of a village earthquake reconstruction committee (Guatemala was rocked by an earthquake in 1976 — 20,000 people died):

Amnesty researchers wrote that "More than thirty bodies were pulled out of the 120-foot gorge ... but farmers who live near the site told me there were more bodies, many more, but that the authorities didn't want to admit as much or go to the trouble of dragging them out. They said vehicles have been arriving at the

---

3   The now well-used word "disappearances" was first coined in Guatemala.

edge of the gorge at night, turning out their lights, engaging in some mysterious activities.

We went down to the bottom of the ravine the next day ... About halfway down the ravine the stench became unbearable. Barely visible in the dim light were piles of bodies. Most were in extremely advanced states of decomposition, but still with remnants of tattered clothing."

The people killed were often, like these villagers, simple peasant folk, but ones who had shown some initiative like running an earthquake reconstruction committee that badgered the government for help, or a co-operative or Church leadership training group. Overwhelmingly it was the incipient peasant leadership that had suffered the most.

The next sizeable group to have been penalised were students and labour leaders. After that, a whole range of professional people disappeared—journalists, clergy, doctors and educators and the cream of the Social Democratic and Christian Democratic parties. Anyone who spoke out and complained, much less organised a formal opposition grouping, was the target for assassination. How did Amnesty arrive at its conviction that the government was in charge of the killings? A series of violent events, observed and recorded by reliable witnesses, all suggested government involvement. The most widely reported mass killing by regular army forces took place on 29 May 1978. One hundred Indians, including five children, were shot dead in the town square of Panzos. The Indians had been protesting about land rights. They were cold-bloodedly shot down by soldiers positioned on rooftops and inside buildings. Townspeople have told Amnesty that mass graves were dug two days before the killings. In January 1979 a group of Indians occupied the Spanish embassy to protest against this and other abuses carried out by the army in El Quiche province. The government, outraged by the protest, ordered the army to attack the embassy. One peasant, Gregorio Yuja Xona, and the Spanish ambassador were the only survivors. Yuja Xona was held under police guard in a hospital, then, without explanation, the police allowed him to be removed. His body was later found, mutilated.

There were a number of occasions when prisoners officially acknowledged to be in police custody were later found dead — for example, 37 killed by garrotte in 1979 and dumped in a ravine. Or the 26 labour unionists who, in June 1980, were arrested by plain-clothes men while the street was closed to traffic by uniformed police, and have not been seen since. The government denied holding them.

There is evidence from one of the very few who have escaped after being picked up. Amnesty International published a taped interview with the former prisoner. He described how he was held in Huehuetenango Military Base and tortured by being pulled up by his testicles and hooded with a rubber inner tube of a tyre lined with quicklime. His testimony was terrifying in its simple directness:

"Before my very eyes they killed three people; they strangled them. The way they killed them was with a piece of rope, a kind of noose, which they put around the neck and then used a stick to tighten it like a tourniquet from behind and with their heads held down in the trough. When they came out, their eyes were open; they'd already turned purple. It took at most three minutes in the water. I also saw that one of these three, a boy, when they threw him down on the floor with his clothes wet, was still moving and one of the officers ordered them to put the tourniquet on him again until he stopped moving. They just showed me the other six bodies and said the same thing would happen to me if I tried to lie to them."

On other occasions, plain-clothes men have been overpowered and found to possess identification papers associating them with the intelligence services. One such event occurred when Victor Manuel Valverth Morales, the student representative on the executive committee of the *Universidad de San Carlos*, was seized at gunpoint in 1980 by two men in plain clothes inside the University's school of engineering in Guatemala City. His assailants did not identify themselves as law enforcement officers or produce a warrant for his arrest. When Morales tried to escape they shot him several times. Other students then came to Morales's assistance and overpowered the attackers and killed one of them.

Students took the dead man's identification card, which showed him to be a military intelligence agent from the "General Aguilar Santa Maria" army base in Jutiapa Province. The second man, who was not harmed, carried an identification card issued by the *Guardia de Hacienda* (Treasury police) for "*Servicio Especial*" (Special Service). The government denied that either of the two men who attacked Victor Morales were members of the security services, but the dead man's widow later confirmed his identity to the press.

I spent four hours in Mexico City with the researcher for Amnesty International Mike McClintock cross examining him on how Amnesty garnered such a wealth of information and established its truth. It was clearly an exhaustive process. External organisations–Church, union and political–who had live networks inside Guatemala fed him with information all the time. He and other members of the small Amnesty team had to evaluate it carefully, learning over time who could be trusted, who had a propensity to exaggerate and who they could ask to double–and even triple-check. When it came to the crucial indictment–that these killings were organised from an annexe to the central palace–Amnesty's method of verification and double-checking indicated to me, an outside investigator, the difficulties and complexities that confront Amnesty.

Amnesty research on the matter required a visit to Washington in 1979 to look at the records and files of US government agencies. With access granted under the Freedom of Information Act, they enabled McClintock to pinpoint key developments in the Guatemalan security apparatus. A 1974 document described the *Centro Regional de Telecomunicaciones* at Guatemala's principal presidential-level security agency working with a "high-level security/administrative network linking the principal officials of the

National Police, Treasury Police, Detective Corps, the Presidential House and the Military Communications Centre". This organisation had built up a sophisticated filing system, listing anyone who might be a potential leader of anti-government movements or a critic of the government. Amnesty also knew from reliable sources that the agency was directed by the joint head of the presidential general staff and military intelligence Major Hecht Montalvan. How could Amnesty confirm, however, that the organisation was something more than a records agency? The research team answered by pointing to the lines of command under Major Montalvan which led directly to some of the killings described above, the capture by dissidents of papers on agents they had overpowered, and denunciations from people who were well known and trusted and who had friends and relatives who worked in the presidential palace.

Montalvan's headquarters was situated in the presidential guard annexe to the National Palace, adjoining the presidential house. I walked around it. Next door, innocently sandwiched into the same block, is the office of the *Obras Pontificiales Misionales* (Roman Catholic missionaries). For a moment I assumed I was at the wrong building, but only yards further on a soldier peered over a balcony and caught my eye; and to his right a television camera monitored the street. On top of the roof were three large telecommunications masts and around the side of the building was the main entrance. In this side street, which on the other side had the door to the president's house, heavily armed soldiers stared at passers-by. Cars with foreign plates or without licence plates at all were parked alongside. A slip of the tongue in a later conversation confirmed that this was indeed the centre of intelligence operations. I was interviewing the head of press information of the army, Major Dominguez. In an aside, he told me he knew that a distinguished Social Democrat politician had been bumped off by a rival. I asked him how he knew. "You see, I used to be military intelligence. But don't tell anyone or the guerrillas will kill me." As casually as I could, I said: "Oh yes, you had your office in the presidential annexe." Surprised, he nodded: "Yes, but remember, don't tell anyone what I've told you."

My loyalty to secrecy in such a situation is, I regret, non-existent. The only task left to do was to confirm the Amnesty investigators' conviction that the intelligence operation did do the killings. Since in Guatemala it is impossible to talk to anyone about politics frankly, I flew to Costa Rica and met some of the Guatemalan exiles who live there. In the relaxed atmosphere of this green and pleasant land—Costa Rica has been democratic for all but a year since it gained its independence from Spain in 1821—it was possible to talk to people who underlined Amnesty's findings. Frustratingly, they were still secondary sources. They insisted that they knew soldiers or officials who had links with the intelligence agency. But only one person I met said he had sources right within the heart of the operation centre.

Some of them knew Elias Barahona y Barahona, who had been the press spokesman of the minister of the interior until he resigned in September 1980. He had told them (and Amnesty had his statement) that blank letterhead stationery of the alleged "death-squads" *Ejercito Secreto Anticomunista* and *Escuadron de la Muerte* was stored in the office of the minister of the interior. According to him, the lists of people to be eliminated were prepared from the records of military intelligence and the national police. They included the names of trade union leaders and peasants provided by the Department of Trade Unions, by the Ministry of Labour and by a number of private enterprises. He also said that an officer in military intelligence had told him that the definitive lists of those to be killed were approved at meetings attended by the ministers of defence and the interior and the chief of the general staff of the army.

Again, it could be argued that this was still a secondary source. Neither Amnesty nor I were able to talk directly to people involved in the command structure of the intelligence agency.

A visit to Washington, DC, however, brought me close to doing so. I called on General Lucas's former vice-president, Francisco

Villagran Kramer, now living in exile in the USA. He had just finished reading the Amnesty report, and although it had been written without any consultation with him, he said it was "absolutely accurate". While he was in power, he said, he learnt how the system worked and was in no doubt that the overwhelming majority of killings were decided in the presidential palace. Nevertheless, he argued that the independent death-squads do play a role, a point which Amnesty in its report seemed to play down. Whenever he wanted to intercede on behalf of a person who had "disappeared", he went to one of three persons — Montalvan, the chief of the president's staff and of intelligence, the army chief or the minister of the interior. These were the three, working through Montalvan, who were responsible for deciding who should be picked up and killed. The fact that Villagran was successful half a dozen times proved to him that those arrested were in the hands of those under Montalvan's command. There was also the telling fact that others who had been picked up in the same swoops never reappeared. His conclusion was reinforced by the scores of army officers who came up to him privately and said: "Mr Vice-President, you're a friend of so-and-so. Do your best to get him out", or "Let him know they're after him". Only if the army were intimately involved in the assassinations could this happen. There was even a man known to him personally, Villagran told me, who was phoned by President Lucas himself and told to get out while the going was good. Although ideological opponents, they were old school buddies and the president was moved to short-cut the normal process of his governmental machine.

The final piece of evidence presented by Villagran was the information given to him by a military officer. According to Villagran, he was senior enough in the military hierarchy to know how the system functioned.

Back in Guatemala it became difficult to keep a sense of perspective and to remember that the deaths were not simply a total to be compared with, say, deaths in neighbouring El Salvador. Moreover, conversations with senior army officers and government officials quickly lulled one into false feelings of security. Their hospitality and bonhomie was disarming. Often enough, probing questions were turned aside graciously and without rancour. Of course, they did not have much to do with the soldiers and intelligence officials who actually carried out the tortures and killings. They gave the orders and the lower ranks implemented them. Blood never touched their hands; it was an antiseptic world that allowed them to make their decisions with the required single-mindedness and ruthlessness.

After a morning of such meetings, I decided to drive the 140 kilometres from Guatemala City to Lake Atitlan, a silver sheen of water lying below three cloud-covered volcanoes. I chartered one of the local fishing boats. It took 80 minutes to reach the village of Santiago Atitlan on the far side. Described by one tourist I had talked to as a "Shangri-La", it certainly gives that first impression. Small houses, inhabited by Indians, rise up the hillside from the water's edge. The men were dressed in broad-striped white trousers cut off just below the knees, the hems decorated with coloured birds laboriously embroidered by their womenfolk. The women had skirts, blouses and shawls of an intricate weave, combining deep reds, browns and yellows, so that when, as I arrived, they poured out of the village church after a mass, there was a riot of colour down the street to the water's edge.

I found the American missionary father, an elderly man, who told me he was standing in for the young parish priest who had returned to the United States after the governor of the province had warned him that his life was in danger. Six months earlier, 25 Indians had been murdered. Four of them ran a small radio station established by the parish; the others were active in the agricultural co-op. "Anyone who shows any leadership potential gets wiped out", the priest told me—an opinion that echoed the Amnesty report.

Did Amnesty itself have any influence? Superficially, one could say, quite the reverse. The killings escalated after Amnesty sent its mission to Guatemala in 1979. Francisco Villagran, for one, felt that Amnesty's pressure in the short run might have been counter-

107

productive. Government officials were obsessed about Amnesty, hardly letting a week go by without denouncing it, just as they made President Carter's human rights policy an object to be scorned and repudiated.

Yet over the long run Amnesty may have been more effective than Carter, who liked to see himself as the "human rights president". For many years, because of the pressure on Washington from Britain, worried about Guatemalan threats to neighbouring Belize, there had been a gradual reduction of arms sales to Guatemala. By the time Carter and his restrictive arms sales policy came on the scene, Guatemala, not having much left to lose, itself decided it would be better off without US arms. Apart then from resisting suggestions from the US embassy to try and woo the Guatemalans to better behaviour by dangling the possibility of renewed arms sales and counterinsurgency training, Carter's pressure did not add up to very much. The occasional critical speech and an attempt, which Guatemala resisted, to send them a liberal ambassador was the sum of it.

Amnesty, on the other hand, had succeeded in alerting a wide constituency to the violence and horror of Guatemala. To take one example, on the basis of Amnesty reports, Church, liberal and union groups in Europe mounted a boycott action over the behaviour of the local bottler of Coca-Cola. In the United States, where the threat of such a boycott was obvious, US labour, liberal and other groups held talks with Coca-Cola management, and eventually put sufficient pressure on the company to force it to buy out its franchise holder on human rights grounds. The manager, apparently, was a personal friend of Colonel German Chupina, director of the national police, and allegedly would simply ring him up if he had a labour problem, and the security forces would be sent in to eliminate the leadership of the local union. (Several union secretaries-general are said to have been killed in this way.) The publicity produced by the Coca-Cola affair in Europe and the United States, together with other reporting, often Amnesty-inspired or at least containing a hard core of Amnesty facts and figures, created an atmosphere that hurt Guatemala economically.

Press reactions to the Amnesty report on Guatemala, following its publication in February 1981, make one understand why the Guatemalan government felt it was the victim of a co-ordinated and widespread attack. The report received blanket coverage: two articles I wrote on the editorial pages of the *International Herald Tribune* and the *New York Times*, a front-page report in the *London Times* and Mexico's *Excelsior* and a long article in the *Economist*. One can perhaps forgive the outburst of the Secretary for Public Relations of the Presidency who told the Guatemalan City daily, *El Imparcial*, that Amnesty "had set out to undermine the prestige of Guatemala's institutions and headed up an orchestrated campaign to damage the image of Guatemala for the simple reason that its government is not disposed to permit the activity of international communism".

The consequence of this kind of bad publicity—there had been a lot before—was that the bottom fell out of the tourist market, once the third largest export earner. Nor was there much foreign investment. A number of US banks closed down their Guatemalan offices, although publicly they gave non-political reasons for doing so. None of this, it must be admitted, had any discernible impact on the government's thinking, so single minded and determined was the regime. Nor did it influence the administration of Ronald Reagan in Washington, but it did give a great deal of succour and support to the opposition. All of the exiles I talked to gained an enormous psychological boost from the Amnesty campaigns. Here they were, citizens of a small country, vulnerable and expendable, being given international attention. The Amnesty publicity did give a sense of assurance to those who were determined to bring about a major change in government policies.

A few years later, in June 1984, I returned to Guatemala, anxious to see if the work of Amnesty had had a cumulative effect. It clearly had not. The Guatemalan government cared nothing about its pariah image in most of the world.

As long as its relationship with Washington was reasonably good—and with Ronald Reagan as president it was more than that—it felt it had nothing to worry about and had all the latitude it wished for to do what it believed had to be done. The new president of Guatemala, General Rios Montt, visited Washington. "We have no scorched earth in Guatemala", he said in an official address, "only scorched communists". In fact, at this time tens of thousands were killed in the counter-insurgency campaign. In July 1982 Amnesty published a paper entitled "Massive Extrajudicial Executions in Guatemala's Rural Areas". In official Washington no one cared, although the *New York Times* published an editorial saying that if even 5 per cent of what Amnesty was saying were true, it would be a scandal.

Reagan was obsessed with communist influence in Central America, to the point that most moral considerations were ruthlessly relegated to the back-burner. Reagan felt it was essential *realpolitik*. As he said on more than one occasion, the close relationship between the guerrillas of Central America and Moscow (never proved) and Havana meant that the red legions (wherever they were supposed to come from) were "only two days' drive to Harlingen, Texas". The Reagan administration persistently tried in its early days to persuade Congress to lift its embargo on military aid to Guatemala (imposed in 1977). It finally gave up after two Guatemalans who were working for the US Agency for International Development in a local project were assassinated. Only in 1985 did it finally manage to persuade Congress to allow military aid to go through, although it is suspected the CIA continued to keep the pipeline open all along. (And Washington actively encouraged right-wing regimes in Argentina, Israel, Taiwan and South Africa to keep the arms flowing.)

On this trip I decided to retrace the steps of my previous journey to Santiago Atitlan. There had been fragmentary reports of clashes between the guerrillas and the army and I wanted to *reconnoitre* the terrain first-hand. I decided to walk the 107-kilometre circumference of the lake, following Indian paths that sometimes took me along the fertile, low-lying lakeside strips, carefully terraced, growing onions, tomatoes, cabbages and avocados in profusion. Sometimes they veered high up in the mountains, where steep cliffs and impossible gorges made cultivation possible only on the upper slopes.

In fact, I saw nothing, apart from realising that this was perfect guerrilla country where hideaways would be hard to discover. No one wanted to talk, apart from the Catholic missionary priests with whom I lodged at night. They told me of what had happened to the young priest I had heard about in Santiago Atitlan on my previous visit. About six months later he had returned from Oklahoma and, true to all his fears, had been murdered. Violence hung in the air. The priests feared it, both for themselves and for their parishioners. They said at the moment things were quiet but it could not last. They were right. Over the years there were many clashes between guerrillas and the army. Nine years later, in December, 1990, the army opened fire on a village protest march in Santiago Atitlan, killing 11 people.

Only as late as 1995 did the beans of Guatemala come to be spilt. The trigger was a US Congressional enquiry into the circumstances surrounding the murder of an American hotel owner in Guatemala. Richard Nuccio, a State Department official, surprised everyone with his frank testimony that the CIA had been aware all along about this, and other political killings in Guatemala. The CIA, he said, had in fact been present in Guatemala, contrary to official US policy, all through the 1990s. President Bill Clinton immediately announced he was opening an investigation to find out why and on whose authority the CIA had been present. Yet the White House did nothing to protect Nuccio, who, having lost his high-security clearance, found himself jobless.

Over the next couple of years more US diplomatic cables and intelligence were declassified. But a breakthrough in getting the full picture did not come until April 1999, when the UN-appointed Guatemalan Commission for Historical Clarification presented its report to Secretary-General Kofi Annan. (The report received most of its financial underpinning from the US and European countries.) A peace agreement between the government of Guatemala and the principal revolutionary movement, the *Unidad Revolucio-*

naria Nacional Guatemalteca, signed in Oslo in June 1994, along with Clinton's decision to open American archives, had made it possible to delve into what had really happened. The Commissioners wrote in the preface that although before they came to write the report "we knew in general terms the outline of events ... none of us could have imagined the full horror and magnitude of what actually happened".

The Commission estimated that the number of persons killed or who "disappeared" "as a result of the fratricidal confrontation" reached a total of 200,000. Seven per cent of the acts of violence were attributable to the guerrillas, 93 per cent to the state. Both the guerrillas and the established institutions of government were blamed for the intensity of the insurgency, the guerrillas for receiving "political, logistical, instructional and training support from Cuba and for treating those who sought to remain distant from confrontation with profound mistrust and even as potential enemies"; the state, for its part, was condemned for its "repressive response, totally disproportionate to the military force of the insurgency ... At no time did the guerrilla groups have the military potential necessary to pose an imminent threat to the State ... The State deliberately magnified the military threat of the insurgency ... The vast majority of the victims of the acts committed by the State were not combatants, but civilians." Worst of all, "a large number of children were among the direct victims of arbitrary execution, force, disappearance, torture and rape, often [being beaten] against walls or [thrown] into pits where the corpses of adults were later thrown. A quarter of all victims were women."

Much of the report reads like an Amnesty report written years earlier, not least in its pinpointing of the supreme role of Guatemala's intelligence system in being "the driving force of a state policy that took advantage of the situation resulting from the armed confrontation, to control the population, the society, the state and the army itself". The majority of human rights violations occurred with the knowledge or by order of the highest authority of the state, the Commission concluded. The report's condemnation of US involvement, however, is perfunctory, merely alluding to how "US military assistance was directed toward reinforcing the national intelligence apparatus and for training the officer corps in counter-insurgency techniques, key factors which had significant effect on human rights violations during the armed confrontation". (It omits to mention that for much of the time this military aid was never approved by the US Congress.) Nevertheless, it was enough to prompt President Clinton to make a public apology during a visit to Guatemala in March 1999 for past US involvement in abuses. At a forum with Guatemalan leaders, Mr. Clinton said: "For the United States, it is important that I state clearly that support for military forces and intelligence units which engaged in violence and widespread repression was wrong." And it led the *Washington Post* to editorialise: "We Americans need our own truth commission."

Yet, if it was not for independent work done by the non-governmental organisation the National Security Archive, we would still be in the dark as to what went on, particularly during the Reagan years, when human rights abuses sharply escalated. The Reagan administration's ambassador to Guatemala, David Chaplin, often prompted his Washington superiors as to what was going on in the country. If less exacting than Amnesty, his embassy's monitors recorded much of the horror of the time.

In February 1984, only one day after Chaplin had sent one of his regular cables to Washington alerting the State Department to Guatemalan government involvement in recent abductions, he was taken aback to hear that the Assistant Secretary of State for Human Rights, Elliott Abrams, a Reagan hard-line appointee had signed off on a secret report to Congress in which he had argued that human rights were improving in Guatemala and that Congress should no longer be inhibited about a resumption of US security assistance. Abrams wrote:

"The Mejia government has taken a number of positive steps to restore a constitutional, electoral process and to address the practice of extra-legal detention ... Failure to provide some politically meaningful sign of support for the efforts being undertaken to return the country to democratic rule and to reduce the human rights violations, will only increase the chance of further political instability. In addition, the US has other strong interests in Guatemala and the region which necessitate a solid, bilateral relationship, including a positive relationship with the Guatemalan military."

In March 2000 Nuccio, the high-ranking CIA official dismissed in 1995 for failing to inform Congress about CIA ties to a Guatemalan colonel linked to over 100 murders, was awarded one of the Agency's highest honours, the Distinguished Career Intelligence Medal.

Typical of the State Department cable traffic of the early Reagan years is a cable that reads: "If General Lucas Garcia is right and the government of Guatemala can successfully 'go it alone' in its policy of repression, there is no need for the US to provide the government with redundant political and military support."

All during the Reagan years the bureaucracy of the State Department's human rights division waged a ferocious propaganda war of its own to discredit the human rights lobbies. One confidential State Department cable, dated October 1982, observed: "After analysing human rights reporting from Amnesty International, the Washington office on Latin America, the Network in Solidarity with Guatemala and the Guatemalan Human Rights Commission, the US Embassy [in Guatemala City] concludes that a 'concerted misinformation campaign' is being waged against the Guatemala government in the United States, by groups supporting the Communist insurgency in Guatemala." The cable accuses the groups of assigning responsibility for atrocities to the army without sufficient evidence, abuses which may never have occurred or may have been propagated by the guerrillas. While the cable concedes that the army has committed violations, it concludes that many of the accusations of the human rights groups were unfounded and that their sources are highly questionable, since they come from "well-known communist front groups".

A month before, Abrams's predecessor as Assistant Secretary of State for Inter-American Affairs, Thomas Enders, had written to the head of Amnesty's Washington office arguing that "many of the incidents [mentioned in the 1982 Amnesty report on extra-judicial executions in Guatemala] cannot be corroborated by other sources such as the press, the army, the police or intelligence information. In fact, the town where one incident allegedly took place (Covadonga) doesn't appear on any map of Guatemala available to the embassy." Amnesty's Guatemalan researcher later said it was "a marvellous occasion" when during a briefing for a visiting delegation from the Organisation of American States (OAS) she could point to the village on the big map she had brought from her office.

It was also a sweet if modest revenge when these same activists from non-governmental organisations could call a press conference in Washington on 20 May 1999 and disclose the existence of an internal logbook compiled by the Guatemalan military that was a detailed record of its death-squad operations. The army log revealed the fate of scores of Guatemala citizens who were "disappeared" by security forces in the period between August 1983 and March 1985, precisely the period when Elliott Abrams had testified that things were getting better. Replete with the photos of hundreds of victims and coded reference to their executions, the 54 page document was smuggled out of army intelligence files and put into the hands of human rights advocates.

How change finally came to Guatemala is not easy to document. It was almost imperceptible. It had many turns and setbacks along the way. Some highlight the end of nearly 20 years of military rule in January 1986. Incoming President Vinicio Cerezo Arevalo immediately committed his government to returning the country to the rule of law. Briefly, there was an improvement, but not many months elapsed before Amnesty noted that "Guatemala is now experiencing a steady escalation in human rights violations". The death-squads, maybe no longer under direct presidential authority, were still active and still in the main composed of police and military agents. Indeed, the amnesties granted by the outgoing military government and then by President Cerezo's government appeared to have facilitated further human rights violations.

It was not until 1993 that Guatemala began to face both its own dark history and the fact that it had isolated itself from a majority of world opinion. Most important, it no longer had an ear in Washington. The turning-point was President Jorge Serrano Elias' (Cerezo's successor) inauguration. He promised to clean house.

But continuing human rights violations, acts of violence in Guatemala and his attempt to seize dictatorial powers enraged Guatemalan public opinion and it turned even the army against him. Into the presidency in 1993 stepped a well-respected governmental human rights advocate, Ramiro de León Carpio. Again, despite its initial promise, the military continued to be recalcitrant and there were a series of high-profile assassinations. Importantly, however, the government signed an accord with the guerrillas, paving the way for a United Nations human rights monitoring team. Carpio also, it can be said, paved the way for his successor, Alvaro Arzu to negotiate a peace settlement with the guerrillas. The peace accord was signed in December 1996. Arzu brought solid progress with a series of land, fiscal and constitutional reforms. He established a fund to help the poor buy land. Arzu also sacked 13 of the 23 generals and replaced them with younger officers. Yet by the end of his term of office it was clear that his reforming zeal had run out of steam.

Why, exactly, the situation changed for the better in the 1990s is hard to pinpoint. It was more the confluence of events than any single person, either in Washington DC, or in Guatemala City. With Reagan's term of office at an end and the Cold War winding down, there was certainly a new way of looking at Central America in Washington. The new president, George Bush, had moved quite quickly, once in office, to end the polarisation in neighbouring Nicaragua and the clandestine support, against the wishes of Congress, for the right-wing guerrillas, the so-called "Contras". This change of direction also sent a clear signal to the military in Guatemala that Washington would not for much longer turn a blind eye to atrocities, although there is no doubt the Bush administration did continue clandestine military support.

Parallel with the change of mood in Washington, but also influencing it, was the Soviet President Mikhail Gorbachev's decision to withdraw Soviet military and economic support for Cuba. This rapidly led Havana to cut back its support for the guerrillas in Guatemala.

Yet beside these major currents of *realpolitik* there was, within Guatemala itself, the process of a generational change. Both in the military and in business, younger elements wanted to end Guatemala's isolation and become accepted by the world outside. At the same time, the ageing guerrilla leadership was attracted by the idea of being welcomed into mainstream politics. The vision of perpetual guerrilladom, ensconced in some hideaway, part sunbaked, part rain-sodden, depending on the season, had less allure as the years slipped by. Under Alvaro Arzu Guatemala had a government, democratically elected, that claimed it wanted to put the past behind it. Centrally directed governmental activism in death-squad murders appeared to be quiescent. Nevertheless, dissatisfied groups, in or close to military intelligence, still took their revenge, whenever they could — as with the brutal murder in 1998 of Bishop Juan Gerardi, who had led the Catholic Church's major project to attempt to document all the human rights abuses over the previous 20 years.

The government, moreover, had been cautious in its welcome of the recommendations of the United Nations Historical Clarification Commission. President Alvaro Arzu made the decision not to receive the report directly, although the previous year he did seek the pardon of the Guatemalan people in a special "Day of Forgiveness". Despite the Commission's charge that the Guatemalan army perpetrated genocide against the country's indigenous people, the government, according to Amnesty, responded to only about half of the suggestions put forward by the Commission and made few, if any, concrete commitments.

The elections of November 1999, the first since the formal end of the 36 year civil war, did not at first sight appear to realise the promise of the peace accords. Indeed, the result appeared to be a set-back for those who thought the peace process might accelerate. The victor was Alfonso Portillo, candidate of the right-wing party, the Guatemalan Republic Front. Although a left-winger, a scholar of Marxist thought in his youth, who spent much of the war in exile in Mexico (where, he admitted, he had shot two men to death 17 years ago—in what he says was self-defence—in a brawl), he ended up attaching himself to the party created by the brutal ex-dictator Gen. Efrain Rios Montt.

A sign of hope was his speech at his swearing-in on 14 January 2000, when he said that the failure to find the killers of the murdered bishop was a "national disgrace". He said he would ensure the murder was solved, no matter where the trail led. A week later the police arrested two military officers, a father and son, colonel and captain, and charged them with the killing. Then in June in a statement President Portillo admitted the state's responsibility for atrocities during the civil war and vowed to prosecute those responsible. "We are doing this today so that the dramatic history we have lived through isn't repeated", he said.

It was not until 1996, under President Alvaro Arzu, that the death squads were finally dismantled. But the momentum towards observing human rights had slowed under his successor, Alfonso Portillo (who was indicted by the US for money laundering and embezzlement). But his successor, Oscar Berger, pushed down on the throttle. The security forces were cut by half. He installed a tough human rights campaigner as ombudsman. Still, such was the danger from free-lance rightists, activists continued to fear for their lives.

Under President Otto Perez Molina who took office in January 2012 the former dictator, Efrain Rios Montt, who ruled for less than two years when he was overthrown in a military coup, was brought to trial and convicted of crimes against humanity and genocide. At the age of 86 he was sentenced to 80 years in prison.

(Presumably his predecessor, General Lucas Garcia, if still alive, would have been tried too.)

Ironically, such are the twists and turns of Guatemala's Byzantine politics, there is serious evidence that Perez Molina, a former military officer, was involved in the same killings as Rios Montt.

A vigorously independent minister of justice, Claudia Paz y Paz who was appointed by Molina's predecessor, Alvaro Colom, Guatemala's first left-leaning president in 53 years, spearheaded top level prosecutions. A former human rights lawyer, this tough, no-nonsense woman put a number of notorious drug dealers and human rights criminals behind bars and indicted Rios Montt. Moreover, her rigorous policies helped lower the horrendous crime rate, one of the world's three worst.

Rios Montt was convicted of ordering the deaths of 1,771 people of the Maya ethnic group. In 2003 he was sentenced to 80 years for genocide and 30 years for crimes against humanity. It is the first time a former head of state had been found guilty of genocide by a court in his own country. Prosecutors said that he had presided over the war's bloodiest phase. They said he turned a blind eye as soldiers used rape, torture and arson against those suspected of supporting leftist rebels. Just ten days later his conviction was reversed. A retrial began in March 2016, accompanied by legal battles over whether he was too old and too ill to stand trial. He died in 2018 while awaiting the court's decisions.

The trial, although ordered by Paz y Paz, partly came about because after the Inter-American Court of Human Rights ruled in 2004 that genocide had occurred in Guatemala and that the Rios Montt regime was responsible for it. Also an international arrest warrant had been issued by a Spanish judge in 2006. Both these events helped change the political and judicial atmosphere.

Interestingly, Rios Montt barely mentioned the United States when he put forward his arguments in his defence. But, as the *New York Times* reported, "Washington's alliance with him was not forgotten in the giant vaulted court room where the current

American ambassador, Arnold Chacon, sat as a spectator in a show of support for the trial". (Chacon was appointed by the administration of President Barack Obama.)

Back in 1983, Elliot Abrams, assistant secretary of state for human rights under Ronald Reagan, once suggested that Rios Montt's rule had "brought considerable progress" on human rights. He also declared that "the amount of killing of innocent civilians is being reduced step by step". Abrams was defending the administration's decision to lift an embargo on military aid put in place in 1977 by President Jimmy Carter, Reagan's immediate predecessor.

Under Reagan, embassy officials had trekked up to the scene of massacres and reported back to Washington the army's line that the guerrillas were doing the killing. According to de-classified diplomatic cables, over the next two years USD 15 million in vehicles, spare parts and arms from the US reached the Guatemalan military. There was military training too. Congress reimposed the ban in 1990 but clandestine aid continued. More aid came from US allies such as Israel, Taiwan, Argentina and Chile. (The latter two ruled by military dictatorships that had carried out terrible human rights abuses themselves.) This secret aid continued under President George H.W. Bush Senior and the early years of President Clinton. Later, the Clinton Administration revealed that the CIA had been paying top military officers through the period.

An international team of prosecutors – the UN-supported International Commission Against Immunity in Guatemala, later known as the CICIG, (financed in good part by the US) – invited in by Attorney-General Claudia Paz y Paz, documented high level corruption going right up to and including President Perez Molina. He was accused of a massive customs fraud network in which corrupt businesses paid bribes in exchange for lower import duties. (Paz y Paz was named by Forbes magazine as "one of the five most powerful women changing the world".)

Paz y Paz persuaded Congress to strip the president of his prosecutorial immunity. Three days later on September 2, 2015, he stepped down. Later the next evening he was arrested and detained in prison until January 2024 when he was released on bond.

In January 2016 Jimmy Morales, a well-known actor in Guatemalan films became president. Some have accused him of having close and unhealthy ties with the military. He has denied that genocide occurred. He disbanded the anti-corruption commission, the CICIG. The Trump Administration's response was muted.

In 2019 the conservative, Alejandro Giammattei, won the presidential election. He appointed a pliant attorney-general, Consuela Porras. Two dozen prosecutors and judges as well as several journalists were either arrested or forced into exile. The government of Joe Biden has sanctioned 36 Guatemalans, mainly officials and businesspeople as "corrupt and undemocratic actors", including Ms. Porras accused of blocking corruption investigations.

In January 2022, the New York Times reported at length on a trial where a court sentenced five former paramilitary members to 30 years in prison for the rape of several indigenous women in the early 1980s during the civil war. But, the paper reported, "While Guatemala has held more trials for abuses committed during the civil war than almost any country in the region, most of the architects of these atrocities have avoided prison."

In August 2022 the Economist reported that Guatemala has the world's fourth highest incidence of child malnutrition. Its biggest export is people—fleeing to Mexico and the US, despite steady growth in the economy. It remains one of the most unequal countries in the world. Three quarters of the rural population live in conditions of abject poverty. Organised crime networks control the country's vast border regions, transforming the country into an ever more fully-fledged narco-state.

It's nearly forty-five years since I first visited Guatemala. Altogether I've made four visits. Mostly I watch it from afar. The war is over. Mass graves piled with bodies are no longer found. There are elections, albeit with much fiddling, and a press that struggles to shout against abuses. But the scales are tilted badly one way.

Justice is too rare. Persecution too common. If the world-wide human rights lobby can have so little benign influence on such a small and inconsequential country, what hope is there for the world at large? I've asked myself this question many times. I remember Martin Luther King's reply when asked a similar question about the war in Vietnam, "If we do not act, we shall surely be dragged down the long, dark, and shameful corridors of time reserved for those who possess power without compassion, might without morality, and strength without sight". We have stood up for our principals in South Africa, Zimbabwe, Tanzania, Brazil and Nigeria and it helped them get to a better place. On the other side of the world, Myanmar and North Korea are particularly hard cases and progress is almost measured in light years. Yet we must persist—non-violently.

Violence carried out by the West would only beget more violence. We know that from the wars that have been led or helped militarily by the US and NATO members—Israel/Palestine, Egypt, Vietnam, Cambodia, Laos, Cuba, Guatemala, El Salvador, Nicaragua, Iraq, Syria, Congo, Somalia, Libya, Afghanistan, Ukraine—to mention the most well-known—that war is very counterproductive. As Martin Luther King said, "We must either learn to live together as brothers or we are all going to perish together as fools. We will never have peace in the world until men everywhere recognize that ends are not cut off from means, because the means represent the ideal in the making, and the end in process. And ultimately you can't reach good ends through evil means, because the means represent the seed, and the ends represents the tree. Means and ends must cohere because the end is pre-existent in the means, and ultimately destructive means cannot bring about constructive ends."

Chapter 7
My friend "Roots" –
Searching for the Bad Boys in the
Caribbean Mountains

Whenever I arrive in a distant place alone my instinct is to dump my bag in the nearest hotel and walk. I never feel comfortable until I've begun to sense that I understand the basic geography, the nature of the people and, in a subconscious sort of way, the escape routes. In certain countries I imagine what would I do if there were a coup or some other dastardly violent act. Who would be my friends? Besides, I've long experienced a chronic loneliness while travelling (although the last few years I've found it much easier), so if I know nobody, I quickly move to remedy the situation.

This time it wasn't someone in my fat address book David Goodhart (the editor of Prospect magazine, an ex-FT guy), says it's the most comprehensive he's ever come across or a friend of a friend who I'd been recommended to phone up. It wasn't a politician or diplomat or newspaper editor whose name I'd gleaned in London. Going to St. Vincent, a small Caribbean Island, had been a rather impetuous decision so I arrived empty handed. I only had, as usual, a small knapsack. So, when I got off the airport bus I started walking.

I intended to chat. It was easy. The town was on the streets. It was carnival time. Every doorway had its loudspeaker. Every store was a bar whether its normal business was selling hoes or clothes. Nobody was still. It was the end of the day and people were getting ready to move their bodies.

The capital of St. Vincent is not much more than a quay by the dock, accompanied by a short main street, part British Victorian and part twentieth century Third World concrete.

Propped up against one of the more garish modern pieces of architectural work were Roots and his friends. I gave them a nod. This was all they needed. "Just say man, whatya need. We can getya anything—a girl? Speed?" I told them I was looking for a cheapish room. Roots, the tallest and strongest-looking of them, took the initiative. Perhaps, he decided, I was a little reserved. He beckoned me over, and then turned on his heel. He ducked into a shack. I followed. I thought he wanted to show me the carnival costumes hanging on the walls, rhinestones and golden glitter in the shape of birds, angels and demons. "Just say, man, what kind of a girl are you looking for. No problem, man". "No Roots", I laughed. "I have a girl friend at home. I just want a bed with clean sheets and a clean bathroom." I stared at the costumes on the wall. The most intricate designs—and high priced too, a cool $200 to $250 each—for becoming for three or four days a being from another world, dressed in glory, feathered from head to toe in the brightest emerald, turquoise, ruby, gold and silver.

We started to look for a hotel. Roots appeared to know half the town and I looked at the people to see how they greeted him. What was in their eyes? Did they look relaxed or was he a hoodlum, a rip-off artiste, that made them avert their eyes? Or just a big boy on the street corner with a loudmouth?

There was something a little incongruous, even on an island where odd visitors come and go every day, for Roots to be accompanied by a white man who was clearly not a student or a hippy. I could see that the people who looked at us couldn't quite get the measure, at least in the four or five fleeting seconds the hellos and goodbyes were made as we flat footed it around the boarding houses.

The first place that had a room turned out to be something of an embarrassment. Partly out of friendship for Roots, partly to please me, the young receptionist gave me a room. But hardly had I put my bag on the bed her mother arrived and explained the room was already let out to some out-of-towners coming in later. I told them not to worry and ordered a drink from their tiny bar. Roots asked for an orange juice and for the next two days we spent together he drank only that. In some of the mountain villages we visited there was only bottled stuff and he would disdainfully refuse to drink. It had to be pure orange juice, straight from a nearby tree. Beer or the ubiquitous coke were no substitute.

Eventually we found a small hotel. I booked in while Roots chatted up the girl behind the desk. I soon learnt that Roots knew most of the young maidens in town, at least enough to say hello to. Of course, every new conversation was a challenge and in a short while I learnt to leave him to it. I'd hurried upstairs and hurried down so as not to keep him waiting. He reprimanded me, as we walked away. "If you had given me five minutes I'd have had my hand on her breast". "Roots", I said, "I'm sorry I cramped your style. You can always come back later. Anyway, you need the darkness to succeed."

We carried on walking. Roots, I realized, was his "nom de plume" or perhaps his "nom de guerre" in his hunt for young ladies. Everyone else called him something more down to earth which I could never quite catch since he and those he met on the street spoke in a rapid patois where the words seemed to be rolled into one extended vowel.

Not only did Roots not drink he didn't appear to eat. He was self-sufficient. He never accepted my offer to eat in a café. Perhaps he was a boy of the earth who lived on digging up and eating raw potatoes and coconuts he scrambled up palm trees to dislodge. Or maybe he just wanted to make sure that I understood he was not accompanying me for financial return.

That evening we went to the town stadium for the semi-finals of the carnival song competition. It was packed and with reason. The contestants had worked for months on their newly minted songs. It was not just the singing. It was pure theatre and spectacle. Indeed, so spectacular were they, I wanted to whisk them off to London and get them to perform side by side with the current hit musical to see if they were as really as good as I, at that moment, thought they were. The costumes were extravagant, the bands large, and the voices soared. They acted out every word in the songs which seemed mainly to be variations on the love theme, the scandal of holes in the road and the incompetence of the politicians. It was exuberance of a high order, rocketing the music into my eyes and ears, overpowering me with a sense of magnificence I normally only feel at the ballet or the opera house. This was more than small island pop. It was art.

I said goodnight to Roots and he said he would come by in the morning. He was at the hotel by breakfast time. Again, he refused to eat. An orange juice was enough.

I had a list of appointments to get through. I was chasing a story for my column – about a school for young delinquents. Briefly, the situation was this. A group of Scandinavian educationalists had set up a reformatory for young boys that the penal system in Europe had despaired of. It took them not only from Scandinavia but also from Britain. I had been alerted to it by an article in the right-wing Daily Telegraph that I picked up from an empty chair by a swimming pool which reported that borstal youths were being sent to "paradise island" at the taxpayers' expense. I was out to discover what was really going on, since I lived in a neighbourhood in London with plenty of bad boys.

I did the routine in town that morning—the British High Commission, the editor of the St Vincentian and the foreign minister. I lent Roots the car. I said we'd leave in 30 minutes. After an hour the owner of the café I was having lunch in wanted to lock up for the afternoon. "You won't see him again", he said. "He's a bad one." Thirty minutes later Roots arrived. He'd done the tour of the town. Now everyone knew Roots had a car.

We set off to find the reform school. Roots asked if he could drive. Our destination was the far end of the island, along the narrow, worn road which linked the coastal villages. Roots was more than ready to go. We went. Fast. And through the villages faster. The small houses clustered at the side of the road. Children and animals freewheeled. This was Roots' moment. He accelerated. For the first two villages I tried to be calm and casual, jokingly suggesting that he was running it a little bit too fine when he almost brushed a wandering goat and then decapitated a disorientated chicken. By the third village my nerves were stretching. By the fourth I was losing my temper "Whose fucking car is this, Roots?" I asked. "Just take it a bit easier, cool it down a little." He slowed. But by the next village the car raced at full throttle again. The sixth, seventh and eighth villages were more of the same. This was a performance.

Roots had many friends. Every third village we would skid to a halt. A child playing at the roadside would be sent inside to announce Root's presence. A young girl would appear. A few quick words were passed and Roots would then accelerate fast, leaving behind what he regarded as a favourable impression.

The dilemma I faced was whether I put my life—and probably those of the goats, hens, pigs and children—before one of Root's rare chances to show his worth. I didn't like to be mean since he had been so generous—giving up his time to be my unpaid and unfed guide. In the end a terrifying lurch that missed an old woman by an inch made me blow. "Fuck it", I said. "Roots, I'm going to drive." My philosophising was cut short. It was now simply life or death. He stopped and moved over without protest.

We continued up and down the backs of protruding mountains, through simple villages of wooden shacks and elementary stone houses. St Vincent has a desolate look, unlike the rugged beauty of Grenada or the gentle orderliness of Barbados, its two touristy neighbours. Its mountains are steep, lurching straight out of the sea and its settlements are squeezed into small coves. It is harsh terrain, unsuitable to agriculture. Houses were surrounded by small gardens of corn and fruit trees of oranges and bananas. The plants looked undernourished. I did not like it.

As we progressed it seemed to become more desolate and forlorn, more windswept and isolated. This was certainly not the "tropical paradise" of the newspaper report.

At last we reached our destination. The school was nothing more than a collection of bare concrete structures on a hillside. Nobody was about. We wandered around until we found a door open and inside what seemed to be the refectory we met four tough-looking white boys engaged in enticing the attentions of a village girl. Maybe *this* is what the Daily Telegraph meant by paradise.

We asked them where the director was and one went off to look for him. The others continued their cooing and wooing. She was a peasant girl with missing front teeth.

A couple of minutes later a young man came in. He was Danish, I think. Without saying hello he announced that the director was away in England and if I wanted to talk to him he could give me his phone number. Taken back, I announced that I had just come from England and the point was to see the institution first hand. "That's all I have to tell you", he said and started to walk away. I followed him and he disappeared into an office. I pursued him, Roots hot on my tail. His office was decorated with pictures of Che Guevara. I read the message. I was the right-wing, capitalist press, about to write another "tropical paradise" story.

"Listen", I said. "I don't make my mind up one way or another until I've seen something with my own eyes". It was the right chord, though it didn't take me very far. "We know the press", he shot back. "You're here just looking for a scandal". It was hopeless. I went into a long debate about how there would have been no resignation of Nixon if it hadn't been for the diligence of the press and about how I'd worked for Martin Luther King. But he was stubborn, unmoveable and kept flapping the piece of paper with the London phone number written on it. He started to get annoyed. "Will you please go? I want you off the premises in two minutes". I was about to boil when Roots interjected. "Look, mister, you wouldn't talk to a reporter like that if he were black." It was a bulls' eye. The man's eyes widened. I laughed a big roar and we tramped out, victorious. The silly left-wing creep, I thought, hung on his own petard by a man, who until that moment, I'd thought was rather thick.

We got into the car and started down the hill. I began to argue with myself. One side of me was burning to write a damning piece. "Secretive borstal with something to hide". The other side of me understood how he felt because when I was a political activist at university, in Africa and in Martin Luther King's civil rights movement I'd distrusted the press for similar reasons. In fact, I first started to write and fight to get articles into newspapers because I thought the truth was not always told.

"Roots", I said. "Mad as we are we've got to find what's really going on. Besides in the capital this morning all I heard was good". We bumped into a black boy and a white boy coming up the hill in a tractor. We stopped them and started to talk. They turned out to be from the slummy Holloway end of Islington, my neighbourhood. One had been sentenced to fifteen years for stabbing another boy at a dance.

They clearly loved the work of farming this barren soil. They didn't miss London. They said they felt they were learning something worthwhile for the first time in their lives. It was the first break they had had. And the world of machine tool workshops and carpentry benches looked rather brighter here than it did in London.

Then further on we came across two members of staff. I did not tell them I was a journalist. We leant out of the car and chatted. They lived here in almost isolation. They were on duty most of the time with only one day off a week. I was impressed by their dedication. In the village a mile down the hill we gave two young local boys a lift and they told us how they had asked if they could be enrolled in some of the workshops and had been allowed to. Now there about 30 local boys who worked alongside the foreigners.

I relaxed. When Roots asked if he could drive I let him, warning him if there was any more speeding I would take over again. The first mile or two were fine. It could not last. He began accelerating. By the next village it was straight down the track, Le Mans. Into the curve, brake, accelerate, spin the tyres, then down into the next village, scattering everything that moved. Then it happened. He took a bend too fast, knocked a wheel against the wall and we ground to a halt. The wheel had been forced right up against the brakes. I waited to see what he did. "Stew in it, Roots", I thought to myself. "I've had enough. You work it out". The minutes ticked by and we stared into space. But then the two boys in the back said they had an idea. They looked, they shoved. They levered with a piece of wood. They got nowhere. I lost patience. "You guys will never solve the brake problem with a buckled wheel. We are going to change the wheel". We did. The brake slipped back into place. The car was working and I was driving.

Dark was coming in and Roots was smelling the pull of the evening. "Can we stop in the next village and pick up a girlfriend?" "Sure", I replied. The girl wasn't ready. She had to change. We lolled around. There was an election meeting going on at the far end of the village and I wandered up, drawn by the razzmatazz blaring out of loudspeakers. A moment later Roots drew up alongside. "I'm just going to the next village to check on another friend. I'll be back in ten minutes". "OK", I said as nonchalantly as I could. The minutes rolled by. The election troupe folded their paraphernalia and disappeared into the night. It was now totally dark and I was alone. "Goddammit", I thought. "Roots has pulled a fast one and has taken the car for a rest-of-the-evening jaunt". Well, I'd been warned by the café owner. I decided to give him another half-hour and then I would resign myself to walking the rest of the way — a good ten miles.

I wasn't in the mood for any new uncertainties. I'd had enough for one day. Then as suddenly as he had departed he reappeared. I got the story. The girl he had been waiting for had not seemed very keen and he suspected the getting changed bit was just a ploy. So he'd raced to choice number two, but that hadn't worked out either. "Let's go", he said. "The Mighty Sparrow is playing tonight. Wanna come?"

When I took the plane out to Barbados late that night I discovered my wallet was gone. I've no idea who took it. I'm sure of one thing — It wasn't Roots.

Chapter 8
Third Way in India – the first interview with the new prime minister, a quiet conversation with Sonia Gandhi and a few words on Kashmir

I was becoming impatient. I had sent both Sonia Gandhi and Manmohan Singh messages by all sorts of different routes but, once the astonishing election results were known in mid-May, Indian politics was a 20 hours a day affair – the principals barely had time to sleep, much less grant an interview to a foreign reporter. For the first few days the question was, would the communists, who had won 7 per cent of the vote, surpassing their own best expectations, join the Congress party in forming a government of the left? Despite arguments in favour by communist heavyweights such as the new speaker of the Lok Sabha (lower house), Somnath Chatterjee, the communists decided against. They would support a Congress government, but from the outside.

Following the announcement that they were staying out – and therefore perhaps making mischief – the Indian stock market had its worst day in its 129-year history. Congress realised that to stop the rot it had to take over the reins of government. To calm the markets, Manmohan Singh, author of India's post-1991 economic revolution, was wheeled out as the likely new finance minister. Five days after the election results came in, APJ Abdul Kalam, the president of India, received Sonia Gandhi to discuss forming a new government and the Congress leadership made it clear, as did the communists, that they expected her to become prime minister. Then the real storm broke. The Bharatiya Janata Party (BJP), the party of the outgoing Hindu nationalist government, announced that it would boycott her swearing-in. As an Italian, they said, Gandhi was unacceptable.

Sonia Gandhi stunned her party and the world when she acquiesced in this BJP veto. She had many reasons. It was clear that her political opponents would continue to use her Italian origins to undermine her government. In such an atmosphere another family assassination could not be discounted. Besides, her ambition if any was to clear the way for the future ascendancy of one of her two children, and her incredible victory had already secured that. Late into another night of debate, it was announced that Manmohan Singh would be prime minister, while Sonia Gandhi remained president of Congress.

I had just flown back from Calcutta – the capital of Indian communist rule – to New Delhi. The next morning the city was quiet for the first time in days. My Indian journalist friends assured me that my messages to my old friend Manmohan were getting through and I would be called in soon. At breakfast I realised that I did not share their confidence, so I cancelled my appointments and took a taxi to Singh's residence in a quiet leafy street where I had spent the morning with him just over a year before. The house was blocked off by a street-long barrier. I circumnavigated it on foot, walked past an Indian soldier who saluted me, and on through an unmanned metal detector and into a makeshift hut inhabited by a man with a phone. I gave my name and five minutes later I was ushered into the garden. Gursharan, the prime minister's wife, was standing there and she whisked me straight into Manmohan's study. I was the first journalist, Indian or foreign, to get an interview on the first full day of him being prime minister.

The house, although large and surrounded by a big garden, was modest inside. Manmohan's study is furnished only with a couple of old chairs, a wicker settee, a desk and bookshelves. Manmohan was sitting there alone, hands resting together. He seemed to be lost in contemplation. "I am so tired," were his first words. "Only two and a half hours' sleep last night." I could see he was overwhelmed by a situation he could scarcely have foreseen.

During the 14 years I had known him, Manmohan has been a man whose heart beats on the left. Although widely known for his term as governor of the central bank and then the finance minister who introduced deregulated capitalism and globalisation to India with stunning results, I remember him first as the secretary-general of the South commission, presided over by Julius Nyerere, the very socialist former president of Tanzania. They wrote a report in 1990, mainly the work of Manmohan, that tore into western capitalism and its exploitative relationship with the Third World. I wrote a column in the International Herald Tribune saying his criticism seemed overdone, even for an (adopted) Swedish social democrat cum green like me, and the Singhs responded by inviting me out for dinner in Geneva, where they then lived.

As we talked now, I became even more aware than before that this brilliant economist had beaten Bill Clinton and Tony Blair to the so-called "Third Way" (neither all blue capitalism nor all red socialism) back in 1991, and that he was determined to use capitalism's energy to improve the prospects of India's poor. "We are centre left," he said. "But we are stealing the clothes of the centre right. Our economic reforms are half incomplete. We have to take them to their logical end. The BJP government was not able to get its act together. It was incoherent, faction-ridden and unable to be effective with its privatisation policies. When we left office in 1996 the growth rate was 7.5 per cent. Under the BJP it slowed to 5.5 per cent." I asked him if he could raise it to 8 per cent, high enough to give China a run for its money. "Eight per cent would require a Herculean effort," he replied. "We have an investment rate of 25 percent of GDP and a savings rate of 23 percent. We need to increase our savings rate and have an investment rate of 28-30 per cent, combined with increased efficiency. This is too ambitious for now. But over five years we can do it. If foreign inflows can rise from the present 0.7 per cent to 3 percent of GDP, it can be done. China has 3.5 per cent. We have to change the mentality of foreign investors. And this we can do if we have stable politics. For now, if we can grow at 6.5 per cent in a sustained manner we can make an impact on poverty and unemployment." (Before he left office 10 years later growth had touched a totally remarkable 10%.)

What is the most important single issue, I asked. "Mass poverty," he replied instantly. "Seventy per cent of our population live in the rural areas and we have to give them good water, primary healthcare, elementary education and good roads." "What about land reform?" I said, knowing that this was the sacred cow of the communists. "We can't have it. It would cause a revolution. Anyway, we are not like the Latin American countries. We don't have the scope for it here. What is important is for sharecroppers to get rights established so they can invest in their land with security. We need to be like the communist government in West Bengal. But we must have fast industrialisation too so that we can draw people off the land."

Although India's spending on its vast conventional forces, nuclear bombs and missiles amount to a fairly small percentage of GDP, India's perpetual confrontation with Pakistan over Kashmir unnerves investors. Indian public opinion seems rather insouciant about nuclear war—80 percent of Indians were not born at the time of the Cuban missile crisis, much less Hiroshima. Manmohan does not share this attitude. For him, peace in Kashmir is urgent business. When I had last seen him in 2002, he and Sonia Gandhi had been up all night finalising an agreement whereby Congress, after Kashmir's first free election in decades, would enter the coalition government together with a local moderate Muslim party, an initiative backed by the then prime minister, Atal Behari Vajpayee of the BJP. The move for a while worked to diminish violence, improve the local human rights situation and prove to Kashmiris that New Delhi is serious about them running their own show.

"The talk of war," Manmohan continued, "is stopping us realising our economic potential. We have an obligation to ourselves to solve this problem. Short of secession, short of redrawing the boundaries, the Indian establishment can live with anything. The constitution of India has a built-in flexibility for legitimate aspirations. In Tamil Nadu in the 1960s we had a problem of would-be secession. Secessionists in the end were elected to government and that ended the situation." This seems to offer Pakistan quite a lot of leeway, although its Kashmiri, al Qaeda-trained ideologues and fighters might not appreciate it.

Then he added an interesting afterthought: "People on both sides of the border should be able to move more freely. We need soft borders—then borders are not so important." "But surely," I said, "whatever you do, the Kashmiris have not forgotten that Nehru promised them a plebiscite?" "A plebiscite," he replied, "would take place on a religious basis. It would unsettle everything. No government of India could survive that. Autonomy we are prepared to consider. All these things are negotiable. But an independent Kashmir would become a hotbed of fundamentalism."

Manmohan was visibly overcome by weariness. His private secretary appeared and ushered me, a cup of tea in his hand, into the old, quite simple, kitchen. Manmohan followed and Gurshran poured two more cups. "I have to go now, Jonathan, there is so much to be done. Do chat with Gursharan while you drink your tea". (I couldn't help thinking when I said goodbye that this homely scene with a journalist and a premier could never take place in China or Russia—or even in Britain or America, come to that.) I repeated to Gursharan what Manmohan had said to me about Sonia Gandhi: that she "is a person who likes to be told things straight—not in the Indian roundabout way. It helps having a European mind. We don't easily get to the point sometimes." "Yes, that's right," she replied, "It's a good balance they have." "So they are going to run this government together?" I ventured. "They will go on working closely. They always have."

I returned to West Bengal. I wanted to get out into the villages and see what Indian communism was all about—to understand what Manmohan meant when he talked of emulating what the communists had done in India's most densely populated state.

Two hours' drive out of Calcutta, I am in the village of Daura, in Howrah district, accompanied by Tirthankar Mitra, a journalist from the Statesman newspaper. The temperature is 47C in the shade and we are out in the broiling sun. I enviously watch the women being towed along by their furiously pedalling husbands as they lounge, gorgeously sari-clad, parasols aloft, on carts attached to bicycles. I have never seen so many bicycles, even in China. I envy too the children splashing in the village ponds. I can't help thinking of Bengal's drought of 1943 and the subsequent terrible famine, one of the worst ever recorded anywhere in the world, in which 3 million people died. "Whatever happened to famines?" I ask my guides. "The last one was 17 years ago. Now we have dams and wells everywhere and where we grew one crop a year we now grow three." Bengal has the highest rice production and highest yields of any state in India.

Everywhere we go, on almost every house and shop, hangs the red flag emblazoned with the hammer and sickle in bright yellow. Next to it I often see a row of Hindu gods or a shrine. I am taken to meet Balaram Khanra, a sharecropper, who grows mainly rice. Back in 1967 he was jailed during the early communist struggle with the feudal landlords. Today he proudly tells me that he is in "peaceful possession" of the land. Before, sharecropping meant giving 75 percent of his produce to the landlord; now it is reduced to 25 percent. He shows me around his brick house — a septic tank was installed in 1986, electricity arrived in 1992 and in 1998 he added a black and white television and an electric fan.

In all the villages, infant mortality, the birth rate and illiteracy are falling rapidly (all indices are much better than the Indian average), and yields are increasing. For 30 years now, agricultural production has been growing state-wide at well over nearly 10% cent a year. The proportion of West Bengal's population below the poverty line has dropped from 50 percent in the 1970s to around a third today and is still dropping. Poverty is now close to the national average.

This peasant revolution began in 1967 when the communists first came to power in coalition with other left-wing and centrist parties. There was resistance from the landlords and, independent of the party, a group of students and peasants in Naxalbari began a guerrilla movement, modelled on Mao and, indeed, financially supported from Beijing. The so-called Naxalites were ruthless, burning title deeds and beheading landowners. The communist authorities eventually put down the uprising, but from then on their task was easier — the landlords were now cowed enough to co-operate with the communist government's land reform plans. As Buddhadeb Bhattacharjee, the chief minister of West Bengal, explained to me in his office in the Writers' Building in Calcutta, "We did three things: we took some land away from the landlords, we gave rights to sharecroppers and for farm workers we imposed a minimum wage of 58 rupees (about 70p) a day."

Land reform, he argued, "should not be a question of capitalism or communism. Look at South Korea, Taiwan and Japan — in all of them, land reform was the key that unlocked rapid economic expansion and industrialisation." The president of the West Bengal chamber of commerce, Biswadeep Gupta, a big industrialist, agrees with him. "There is now an enormous economic savings surplus in our rural areas. In rural India this state has the highest. This is going to drive growth for investors. Now we are selling things that once were considered unnecessary for living, everything from soap to motorbikes."

Will Manmohan Singh push for such land reform elsewhere in India?" I asked Somnath Chatterjee, the communist Lok Sabha speaker. "We are giving Singh unconditional support. And we know that he is putting a lot of emphasis on the rural poor. About 700 farmers have committed suicide this year because of indebtedness. There is no alternative to land reform. Of course, it will depend on the political make-up of each state. We don't expect to see it in BJP states. But Congress must make an adjustment to coalition policies."

The communists might have achieved more of their objectives if they had entered the government. Promising to vote with it gives them some influence but not as much as if they had taken the risk of losing some of their identity, and thus votes, in the next state elections.

Judging from what Manmohan told me then, he would take steps towards the communists: giving sharecroppers greater security and possibly even the minimum wage for farm labourers. But he won't move to strip titles from big landlords, as they are one of Congress's important constituents. This is similar to the policy advocated by Professor Roy Prosterman of the Rural Development Institute at the University of Seattle, one of the world's greatest authorities on land reform. On a trip to England he had come out to see me at my home in Oxford. "There are not many columnists interested in the dry details of land-reform", he joked as I met him off the train. "Worth a trip!" West Bengal's reform, he told me, has been a stunning success, but he recognises the political and financial difficulties of spreading similar legislation to the rest of India. For him the worst problem is the landless, who make up about 11 per cent of rural families. He believes it is possible to give these people "homestead plots," a fraction of a hectare sufficient for a garden, trees and a few animals. "This would require less than one third of 1 percent of India's arable land, transforming our assumptions about the affordability of land reform."

I asked Bhattacharjee how far the communists would bend in supporting Congress? Over the last ten years, they had changed from a party of absolutist dogma to one of surprising pragmatism. "We are globalisers now," says Bhattacharjee. "We have been to Shanghai and seen that it works." He is very critical of the old communist policy of supporting militant unionism, which regularly closed down whole businesses, often violently. "Now we say labour productivity is not just the responsibility of management. The unions must co-operate too." He was determined to woo the multinationals and especially the information technology sector where he was convinced Calcutta could overtake Hyderabad, given its large numbers of well-educated people (bequeathed by the educational institutions of the Raj) and the lowest crime rate of any major city in India (and indeed in the world). West Bengal's fiscal deficit is large and interest payments on debt the highest in India, but it now has one of the highest rates of growth of the Indian states Moreover, relations between Muslim and Hindu are harmonious. The BJP does not do well here.

The communist party swept the board in Calcutta, a city in which they usually struggle. Despite its popularity, it cannot resist the temptation to intimidate opponents. Bhattacharjee still hangs a portrait of Lenin in his office, explaining, "I believe in class. I don't think capitalism is the last chapter of civilisation."

So this is Congress's coalition partner. Ravindra Kumar, the editor of the liberal Statesman—the one local mouthpiece that is consistently critical of the communist fiefdom—told me he wondered if the communists would keep Congress in power for a full five-year term. He blamed them for the big stock market crash and says that they should have "explained their position more articulately." Only a few days before the election Bhattacharjee had called Singh "the torchbearer and lackey of the World Bank and IMF."

Singh was going to have to deal with the communists' ambiguities. He told a post-election press conference: "Life is never free from contradictions." He added: "Our friends on the left have a different perception of past economic policies, but they are also great patriots and that patriotism and burning desire to make this century the Indian century is something I see common to all Indians."

There was room for manoeuvre, as Kumar explained to me. "The fact that Congress has already watered down its privatisation policy to please the communists shows that Singh is flexible. But this is not imperative for economic reform. Reform is about opening up competition, cutting down controls and the Marxists these days won't object to that."

The big question was whether Singh could set India on the path to overtake China in a decade or two. India had—and still has—a lot

going for it that China does not. Apart from its thriving democracy and free press, it has world-class companies, especially in information technology, biotechnology and pharmaceuticals. It has
the intellectual capital of its emigres returning from Silicon Valley.
Its banking system has relatively few underperforming assets. Its
capital markets operate with greater efficiency than China's.
Above all, it has the rule of law. As one western banker said to me,
"China progressed so fast because it had no law. But now India
will overtake China because it has law."

Ten years later Congress lost the election to the BJP. Corruption, a
rise in inflation and a slowing of the fast economic growth it had
achieved during most of its term were the issues that brought it
down. But in those ten years the number of poor had been halved,
health care and education for the poor had improved steadily. The
middle class had become more sizeable than the population of
"old Europe". There was almost one mobile phone per head of
population and everyone now has a biometric ID card which
among other things enables the poor to receive government subsidies direct into their bank account without going via often corrupt middlemen.

India could be the power that dominates the second half of this
century. I, for one, would rather India than China

Sonia Gandhi was the underestimated candidate. It is not hard to
see why. She had everything against her — her origins (Italian), her
religion (nominally Catholic), her education (modest) and, not
least, the fact that this shy woman pales by comparison with her
murdered mother-in-law, Indira Gandhi, the master politician.
Even some of her staff were dismissive, calling her Kungi Ku-
reya — Hindi for a mute doll.

Yet when, a few months before her surprise election victory, in a
very rare interview, I met the 57-year-old head of the Congress
party — and, along with Prime Minister Singh, the key figure in the
new Indian government. She came across as a woman who was
not at all anxious at the prospect of ruling over 500 million males.

When I arrived I didn't get a handshake. Surprised, I decided to break the ice by asking my last question first. "May I ask you a very personal question?" Quietly but quickly the answer came back: "Yes." "Isn't it difficult to go into the centre of the maelstrom of Indian politics knowing all you do of its dangers and the terrible toll it has taken with two assassinations in your family? (Her mother-in-law, Indira Gandhi, and her son, also prime minister, Rahul.) Are you really at peace with that?"

"I am at peace. I have thought it through," she replied.

"How did the pull of politics overcome your inhibitions? You had long said you would never go into politics."

She replied: "At the time of the 1998 election Congress was in serious difficulties. We were divided. Senior members of the party who had tried to persuade me before came to me again. My children were grown up. I agreed. Moreover, I feel very strongly about India being a secular state. By secular state I mean one that encompasses all religions. The present government doesn't stand for that. It is important that Congress is in power."

She looks surprised when I ask her about her own religious convictions. "I'm not religious. My family never was. My father never went to church; my mother did but not every week. I got sent away to boarding school so I suppose that had its effect too."

"So on what principles do you draw when you make moral decisions, in family life or in politics?"

"I suppose Catholic values are at the back of my mind," she replies without needing to pause to weigh what she is saying.

"How would that affect a decision whether or not in a crisis to use nuclear weapons? Could you press the button?" She grimaces but doesn't answer.

I break the silence recounting how when Zbigniew Brzezinski was President Carter's national security adviser I asked him this question and he had replied strongly in the affirmative, saying that otherwise there was no point in deterrence and that he would like to see the Soviet Union suffering the same destruction that it was about to inflict on the United States.

"But Robert McNamara has a very different view on the value of nuclear weapons," I added.

"I like that man. He's been here a couple of times for seminars. I have learnt a lot from him," she says.

The mood has changed. The tension has dissipated. For the first time she is looking me in the eye. I can see she wants to talk about the dilemma of nuclear weapons but time is pressing. We agree to talk about that in our next conversation. Meanwhile she is keen I send her a copy of the McNamara book I had mentioned in which he argues for forsaking the nuclear weapons he had advocated when he was Secretary of Defence during the Kennedy and Johnson presidencies. She asks me not to write in detail about this part of the conversation, but I am left with the feeling of a moral soul who will not take a step towards war with the equanimity of her mother-in-law.

We end up talking at length about Indira Gandhi, and I recounted a couple of the funny political stories she told me in one very long interview.

She raises her hands ever so slightly. My time is up. As I stand to leave I am moved to tell this obviously solitary and even disconsolate woman what I've never in FIFTY years of reporting the world told another politician: "I know you are a good person. I can see that. I think India will be in good hands with you and Manmohan at the helm. Can we keep talking?" She nods and holds out her hand.

****

The issue of Kashmir has dominated Indian foreign policy ever since colonial India was partitioned into predominantly Hindu India and Moslem Pakistan in 1947. The British left Kashmir with a majority Muslim population and a Hindu ruler. Both Pakistan and India claimed this beautiful piece of Himalayan real estate.

The conflict has led to three wars. President Clinton observed that a nuclear war was a real possibility.

India missed its great opportunity to settle the burning dispute while the military president, Pervez Musharraf, who ruled Pakistan from 2001 until his overthrow in 2008, was in power.

According to diplomats I talked to, both British and American, in New Delhi and Islamabad, a deal was tantalisingly close. One British ambassador told me that the main barrier to a deal was "psychological" and that India had to make very few concessions to make a final deal.

If Musharraf wasn't prepared to give away the store, the Pakistani compromises came close to it. But India, despite the seemingly friendly diplomacy of Foreign Minister Pranab Mukherjee, the unwarlike prime minister, Manmohan Singh and, in the background, another unwarlike figure, the chairwoman of the Congress Party, Sonia Gandhi, couldn't bring itself to go the extra mile.

Observers had different explanations for Indian intransigence — that Musharraf was trying to force the pace; that the Indian army, the intelligence services and senior bureaucrats in the foreign ministry were resisting an accord; that the leadership had not made an effort to educate the electorate as Pakistan's had done; that the prime minister was weak and over preoccupied with the economy; that his (highly successful) attempt to lower the grinding poverty in the rural areas was also a preoccupation; that the time consuming nuclear deal with the U.S was critically important; and that India rather liked the status quo, since stubbornness fitted in with its self-image of being the sub continent's super power. There was also the failure of the George W. Bush Administration that was, in Singh words, "loved" by India for pushing a deal through Congress that lifts the long-standing embargo on selling nuclear materials and reactors to India. America could have used the muscle that the nuclear deal gave it to help push India to sign on to Musharraf's magnanimous offer. It didn't.

Then after his re-election Prime Minister Singh unexpectedly found himself riding high. Not only did Congress win hands down, but the grumbling that Singh was a weak prime minister had disappeared. Singh might still say, as he said to me eighteen months before, "How can you expect me to push a peace deal when militants are coming from Pakistan every few months to set off bombs in India?" Needless to say, the big bombing in Bombay in 2010 reinforced his argument. But when I repeated this in my interview with Musharraf, he responded sharply. "I don't agree with his way of looking at it. If everyone in the world looked for calm and peace before reaching a solution, we would never achieve peace anywhere. It is the political deal itself that can produce calm. Bomb blasts are a result of the problem. Let's not put the cart before the horse."

Musharraf had his own reasons for compromising and so did his successors, the democratically elected president, Asif Ali Zardari, and Prime Minister Nawaz Sharif. The conflict has led to Pakistan-based guerrillas fighting for a free Kashmir (which Pakistan's intelligence service has long secretly supported, although much less these days). In turn, these militants have given aid, men and advice to the Taliban in Afghanistan. For their part, the Taliban have perhaps given succour, or at least provided an example, to other militants that tried to kill Musharraf and that on the eve of an election murdered Benazir Bhutto as she campaigned to be prime minister.

Can India go on stalling, tie down the Pakistani army on its joint borders and watch Pakistan perhaps tear itself apart?

The official Indian stance is to claim the whole of Kashmir, including that part long occupied by Pakistan. But in the earlier negotiations India did concede in principle the notion of "soft borders" — that has already allowed limited bus travel across the "line of control" that divides the two halves. India has hinted at consideration of the abolition of this "line of control", and at the same time accepting the division of Kashmir, the withdrawal of Indian soldiers and separate autonomy for the two parts of Kashmir. Some have called this the "Irish solution".

Prime Minister Singh should have stepped forward and made the historic compromise. He didn't and the great opportunity for peace evaporated in the mists on Kashmir's Himalayan mountains.

Chapter 9
Penetrating the Thoughts of
Pakistan's Military President

Pakistan was the hub of the Anglo-American/NATO war against the Taliban and al Qaeda. Britain's embassy in Islamabad is its largest in the world. And the city has for decades been full to the brim with American spies and senior military people. But the truth is that the war in Afghanistan had long been going badly, before the new president of the US, Joe Biden, finally pulled the plug in 2021. The Taliban long had the upper hand, funded by proceeds from poppy-growing, which they now encourage in a reverse of the policy pursued when they were in power the first time (back then, it was un-Islamic).

In the course of a wide-ranging, two-hour conversation in his office in the presidential palace in July 2006 Pervez Musharraf, military strongman of Pakistan, made no effort to persuade me that the Taliban and al Qaeda were being defeated or that the war in Afghanistan was going well. There was an absence of bravado and an apparent openness to new ideas—such as talking more formally to the Taliban and Al Qaeda and even buying up the poppy crop.

Indeed, Musharraf is the first world leader to tentatively back the idea of western governments buying the Afghan poppy crop to stop it reaching the drug barons yet without impoverishing the farmers. "Buying the crop is an idea one could explore. Pakistan doesn't have the money for it. We would need money from the US or the UN. But we could buy up the whole crop and destroy it. In that way the poor growers would not suffer," he told me.

The idea of buying the Afghan poppy crop was first floated in 2005 by Emmanuel Reinert, head of the Senlis Council, a development think tank. The council's proposal would solve two world problems in one blow. First, it would help deal with the world shortage of medical opiates, which according to the World Health Organisation is causing a "global pain crisis." Second, it would prevent the opium farmers of Afghanistan being driven into the arms of the Taliban.

Western soldiers sent to Afghanistan to fight the war on terror were also, at least intermittently, waging a war on drugs that required the destruction of an important part of the Afghan economy The 2017 crop was worth $1.4bn, equivalent to almost half the country's GDP. According to a UN report, opium is being produced in 28 of Afghanistan's 36 provinces, especially in the south; and Afghan opium makes up 92 per cent of the world's supply. The Afghan opium harvest is 50 per cent bigger than in 2005, and 3,000 per cent bigger than in 2001 when the Taliban were still in charge. As lead G8 nation on the Afghan drugs trade, Britain has spent millions of dollars years trying to reduce opium production, but only about 38,000 acres out of a total of 430,000 under cultivation were destroyed last year. Even at the end NATO still lacked a proper strategy for dealing with the opium question: troops from different countries pursued different tactics. And with opium paying up to 12 times more than conventional farming, it is not surprising that many small farmers looked to the Taliban for protection from western troops.

The Americans are very unlikely to back an official common agricultural policy-style purchase. Moreover, there are many practical problems with the idea of such a purchase. If the price were set too high, it might encourage even more farmers to grow opium poppies. If it were not high enough, they would go on selling at least some on the black market. Nevertheless, they would probably rather sell their crop legally than to the mafia. Musharraf nodded as I listed some of these problems, and said, "Look, let's analyse it, let's cost it and see if it is practical."

When my long-time friend, Sartaj Aziz, former finance and foreign minister of Pakistan, read the article I wrote for Prospect magazine suggesting this he wrote me an email backing me up, saying a "Buy" campaign could be done on a trial area in one province to see if it worked. At my suggestion he wrote this down as a letter to the editor. It was published, but neither of us was able to trigger a public debate. The Taliban today seem to have a policy of clamping down on poppy growing, officially banning it in April 2022. But the market doesn't yet seem to be disrupted. According to the UN since the Taliban took power opium cultivation increased by 32%.

At the time I was talking with Musharraf the presidents of Afghanistan and Pakistan were besieged. President Hamid Karzai appeared to realise that the western forces were losing ground to the Taliban and that he could do little about the infiltration of fresh fighters from Pakistan. In 2003, Musharraf sent 80,000 troops into Waziristan, the semi-autonomous tribal area that borders Afghanistan, in an attempt to flush out Taliban and al Qaeda fighters. This was partly the result of western pressure, but his troops took such a battering that Musharraf sued for peace, withdrawing the army in return for an agreement that local tribal elders would resist Taliban encroachments.

Meanwhile, popular support in Pakistan for the militants appeared to be growing. As Tariq Fatemi, a former Pakistan ambassador to the EU, wrote in the Karachi newspaper, Dawn, brute force tactics which have killed women and children and destroyed homes have been counterproductive. "The impression has gained ground among the tribes that we are oblivious to their lives and interests." At the Pakistani election in 2002, the religious parties, which had never in the past been politically significant, won 11 percent of the vote. Unsurprisingly they won office in Baluchistan and North-West Frontier province, both provinces that border Afghanistan.

The Pashtuns, one of the world's most adept fighting peoples, are found on both sides of the border — making up almost half of Afghanistan's population of 30m and about 17 percent of Pakistan's population of 169m. They have been the standard-bearers of Afghan nationalism ever since the Afghan state came into being 250 years ago. Although they have a strong religious and ethnic identity, the Pashtuns also have a long tradition of inter-tribal rivalry. (The Taliban are almost exclusively Pashtuns, but by no means all Pashtuns are Taliban supporters.) They close ranks against the invader—British, Soviet or American—and then turn to fighting among themselves when the threat passes.

The current cycle of violence will only be ended by negotiation. A jirga (tribal council), which brought together the Taliban, Kabul, Islamabad and Pakistan's northern tribes, would require a cease-fire. And the Taliban would insist on a timetable for the withdrawal of Nato troops. But when I asked Musharraf, "Why don't you talk to your enemies, the Taliban and Al Qaeda?"—he does not slap the idea away. Pakistan has, after all, already been talking to the Taliban informally in the tribal areas and elsewhere.

I pressed on. "Perhaps", I said, "the Afghan Taliban should not be feared as much as they are. Al-Jazeera's recent interview with Mullah Omar suggested that the Taliban leader is distancing himself from Osama bin Laden. No Afghan has been directly associated with any terror attacks in the west. Bin Laden, assuming he and his men are in Pakistan, can no longer easily finance or mastermind terrorism from a remote cave. He could be finished off by careful police work. Al Qaeda operatives are paying locals in dollars for protection, as you (Musharraf) yourself told me. That makes a kind of paper trail. As for the harsher side of would-be Taliban rule, let Pashtun culture work on that over time. The Pashtun ethos does not promise democracy, but a sort of personal autonomy and equality."

"You have a point there, we must think about it," Musharraf says. I also suggest that he engage in less "bang bang" and more economic and social development in the alienated, impoverished border villages that lack schools and clinics. He did not demur.

Before visiting Musharraf, I had had an off-the-record conversation with my old friend Manmohan Singh when he said to me, how can you expect me to push a peace agreement on Kashmir when militants are coming from Pakistan every few months to set off bombs in India? No leader can be too far ahead of public opinion.

But when I put this to Musharraf, he responded sharply: "It is the political deal itself that can produce calm. Bomb blasts are a result of the problem. Let's not put the cart before the horse."

Good point, especially since the general atmosphere between the two countries is now quite benign—witness when I was visiting Islamabad the meeting between the two foreign ministers, where they and their delegations talked and dined with each other like old friends. At my table it was all bonhomie.

Moreover, much has been achieved on other important issues—border delineation in Sir Creek and the Siachen glacier, together with the opening of crossing points on the "line of control" that divides Kashmir between the two countries. Khurshid Kasuri, Pakistan's foreign minister, told me over lunch in Lahore that the Siachen dispute "could be solved within days."

Revealingly—it was normally denied on the Pakistani side—Musharraf did not deny that various extremists are active from inside Pakistan. Nor did he deny that al Qaeda and the Taliban have hideouts in Pakistan. But he emphasised that it does not help to blame Pakistan, as the US intelligence chief, John Negroponte, had recently done, for not going all-out to unearth the al Qaeda and Taliban terrorists. "We are doing more than anybody," he insists. "Why doesn't the US blame Mexico for sending illegal immigrants to the US? Some problems are not easily solved. We can't send the army into the narrow alleyways of the refugee camps—in Quetta there are 40,000 people in just one camp—and start fighting to capture the militants who hide out there. The damage to innocents would be terrible."

Musharraf's view is that the terrorists now operating out of Pakistani territory—whether fighting in Afghanistan, setting off bombs in India (the latest big outrage killed 186 people in Mumbai) or spreading terrorism around the world—are hangovers from the past miscalculations of outside powers. The US, having

151

armed and used the Taliban to defeat the invading Soviet army, left Afghanistan to its own devices with the militants fully armed. Britain walked away from India and Pakistan leaving Kashmir unsettled. But Musharraf does not mention that one of his predecessors, Zia ul-Haq—another general who staged a coup—is partly responsible for building up the power of these extremists, and that as an influential military leader he too did his bit to help them. Now, however, Musharraf fears that if he clamps down too hard he will lose all influence over the militants, who would simply melt into the mountains—and continue trying to assassinate him. They've already tried to a number of times. How can one reasonably say he is on their side?

The reality is that if India willed it, Kashmir could be settled fast. That would help diminish the power of the extremists inside Pakistan. Does Singh weigh that in his calculations? I think not sufficiently.

Musharraf was no saint, but he impressed a wide range of people—even those who oppose army rule—with his integrity. It was unlikely he was playing a complicated double-game, as some suggest, in which he appeared to repress terrorists but privately nurtured them, or at least turned a blind eye. As UK Prime Minister David Cameron said on a visit to Pakistan, "the country faces both ways". Perhaps we should have worked on the basis it didn't.

Chapter 10
Oh! Kolkata

If we are discussing "Oh! Calcutta" or, to give it its proper name, "Oh! Kolkata", let's strip! Strip away the accumulated layers of being since the East India Company set up shop in 1772 and the British made it in 1858 the capital of its Asian domain. Strip away the only thing that most of us can recall about it—the "Black Hole" where 146 British and Anglo-Indian soldiers were incarcerated in a small and filthy dungeon until 123 died of suffocation. Strip away what almost every journalist and novelist who has written about Kolkata has said. Geoffrey Moorhouse thirty years ago in his book "Calcutta", still the standard text on the city, describes a city of warts and scabs. To give him his due, once or twice he hints at an alternative view: "The imperial residue of Calcutta, a generation after Empire ended, is both a monstrous and marvelous city. Journalism and television have given us a rough idea of the monstrosities but none at all of the marvels." Mother Teresa's good works haven't helped the image much—the dead and dying and the selfless, loving nun standing between them and the horror outside the order's refuge.

Kipling was the Victorian master of words on India. He visited Calcutta as a newspaper correspondent down from the Punjab and wrote a series of essays about it entitled, "The City of Dreadful Night". His poem on the city is one all those British schoolboys and girls studying English literature know about it:

"Thus the midday halt of Charnock—more's the pity!—
Grew a City
As the fungus sprouts chaotic from its bed
So it Spread
Chance-directed, chance-erected, laid and built
On the silt
Palace, byre, hovel—poverty and pride—
Side by side;

And, above the packed and pestilential town,
Death looked down."

Robert Clive, founder of the British Raj, described Calcutta as "the wickedest place in the universe". One and a half centuries later V.S Naipaul in his cynical classic, "An Area of Darkness", wrote that "Calcutta was dead. Partition had deprived it of half its hinterland. But Calcutta's death was also of the heart. With its thin glitter, its filth and overpopulation, its tainted money, its exhaustion, it held the total Indian tragedy and the terrible British failure. Here the Indo-British encounter had at one time promised to be fruitful. Here the Indian renaissance had begun—so many of the great names of Indian reform are Bengali. But it was here, too, that the encounter had ended in mutual recoil. Once Bengal led India, in ideas and idealism; now, just fifty years later, Calcutta, even to Indians, was a word of terror, conveying crowds, cholera and corruption." Jawaharial Nehru, the first prime minister of independent India, called the city "the nightmare experience".

The observations by sharp and talented writers writing today convey much the same sense of despair. Paul Theroux in his novel of 2009, "A Dead Hand—A Crime in Calcutta", writes of it as "a city of deformities", a city "in its exhalations of decay. The old splintered and pitted buildings looked eaten away and incomplete. The cracks showed through the peeling paint, the dirty shutters, the windows opaque with dust, the dead bulbs, the flickering neon, the wobbling rickshaws and beat-up taxis, all like a dream of failure."

I first arrived in Kolkata 50 years ago on my way back from observing the aftermath of a coup in South Korea against the country's harsh but effective dictator, Park Gung-hee. The abiding memory of Seoul still with me today was the teams of women carefully picking up the cigarette stubs thrown out of the train window onto the tracks. I flew from perfect cleanliness to muck, grit and slime.

Safe and cosseted in Kolkata's sole up market hotel, I dumped my bags and went for a walk. It was evening and the few street lights illuminated the grotesque shapes of buildings worn and splattered over centuries. In the eerie light I could see the sleeping bodies of families that occupied most of the pavements. There was barely any traffic apart from the frail, underfed and overworked men pulling rickshaws. I turned a corner and went up an alleyway. There I saw an apparition that has stayed with me all my life – an old man with an enormous pile of used toilet paper (from the posh hotel?) tearing the "clean" bits from the soiled half and making a smaller heap. What he was going to use it for I have no idea.

The next day a Catholic priest showed me around one of shanty towns that stretched for miles. Raw sewerage in shallow creeks wound its way round the "packed and pestilential" dwellings. "Slum Dog Millionaire" brought the horror to life for today's cinema goers, but that was shot in Mumbai. Dominique La Pierre wrote in 1985 a best-selling book "City of Joy" (still sold by street booksellers) in which he gives a close up of life in these holes and horrors of Kolkata. Its message is the sublime way people cared for each other, the profound sense of community; the ability, despite all adversity, to smile and the children to laugh as they make up games racing round the shacks and jumping over the rivulets of sewerage; the people lining up to use dirty toilets, but allowing the old and infirm to pass to the front of the queue; and when needs be sharing their meagre rations of food with a destitute neighbour.

The second time was for three days twenty years ago when I concentrated on prying two years' worth of payments out of The Statesman, a once famous, but now deteriorated, national newspaper – with filthy toilets to match. (I always think toilets tell one a lot about the morale of a place – and Kolkata's public toilets, which I have visited, are sparking clean!)

One of its journalists agreed to educate me when I asked about the shanty towns and the families sleeping on the streets. She took me out to where the biggest shanty town used to be. It was no more. All had been rehoused in flats – as had families from the other shanty towns. She confirmed what I could see for myself – there were very few families sleeping on the pavement. You couldn't film "Slum Dog Millionaire" in Kolkata. The then ruling communists had done a good job. In no other city — apart from those in Kerala in the south where the communists also rule — has so much been done for the poor. The former Prime Minister, Manmohan Singh, whose heart has always beaten on the left, once told me in his kitchen over a cup of tea that West Bengal was the state he most admired. It is reported to be India's safest city.

The next time I visited was the time of the election that brought Prime Minister Manmohan Singh and Congress Party Chief, Sonia Gandhi, to power. I could see there were fewer rickshaws and the men who pulled them better fed. They were replaced by very clean — washed every day — yellow taxes that blared their horns every minute. And the street lighting had improved.

Five years later I lived in Kolkata — lured by the former editor of the op ed page of The Statesman. We got to know each other at the time of the election when she was editing my syndicated International Herald Tribune column. She was then "happily married". We had lunch a couple of times and a few cups of tea. And that was that, apart from the enormous goodbye cuddle she gave me. She got in touch with me again five years later after her husband had left her for another woman. Divorce is exceedingly rare in West Bengal, but he wanted it. We renewed our brief friendship by email. After a couple of months of correspondence when we became more intimate by the week she asked me to visit her...

Maybe I look at the city through rose tinted spectacles. But even that critical eye, Geoffrey Moorhouse, could notice in the neighbourhood of Chor Bagan (Thieves' Garden), "an acre with a Palladian mansion set square in the centre. This could easily be a luxurious pocket in Rome, and there is a fountain in the garden that would not be out of the place in the Piazza Navona or at the bottom of the Spanish Steps; it has Neptune figures brandishing conch cells with indeterminate water beasts gaping at them from the surrounding pool and four nubile maids upholding a classical urn on top of the central column."

At the heart of this city of 14 million souls – the twelfth largest in the world – is the Maidan, a great expanse of parkland, larger than New York's Central Park. The city is covered in parks, mostly smallish squares suitable for cricket or football and, near where I lived, a park surrounding a sizeable lake that took me every morning 45 minutes to circumnavigate at a fast-walking pace. The parks, I was told, used be run down and full of detritus. Today, many of them are spick and span, often voluntarily kept clean by a nearby big business doing its social bit in return for a signboard.

The Maidan stretches on as far as the eye can see. An ancient, lumbering, tram takes you from one end to the other, past the ubiquitous boys playing cricket, the goats, cows and horse drawn carriages wandering by, past the perfectly kept botanical garden, a mass of flowers all year round, and then up to near the Victoria Monument, the dream of the Viceroy, Lord Curzon. It is a giant of a building, built by the British in white marble. It is now a popular museum. All this expanse of park is fairly quiet during the week, but at the weekend it is taken over by families eating picnics and local teams competing at cricket.

The famous, always packed, recently restored, cricket ground, the Eden, lies at one end. Once I went to watch India playing South Africa. I talked myself into the press box and found myself in a seat with a startling view over the greensward. This wasn't like watching cricket from the stands of Old Trafford when I was a boy. This was as if I had been helicoptered over the pitch. Three young women – two white and one Indian – chatted away, barely noticing the game. I asked the one sitting near me if they were the girlfriends and wives of the South African players. "Yes. We are!" she said and we talked a bit about where the next match was and who was likely to win this game. This woman sat alongside me and the other two sat behind so I was partly talking over my shoulder. After a while I turned round to take a look at them – to my surprise the Indian one was in purdah. Her eyes shone and I could see that she was probably very pretty. Clearly, judging by their chat, she had no trouble in being one of the girls. She was the wife of South Africa's star batsman who was beating the Indian team into submission.

The city is full of grandeur and surprises. I didn't see it on my early visits, perhaps because it was all laden with dark dirt and discolouring fumes. Today it is being cleaned up and the Raj's buildings are being scrubbed and painted into a new life. The headquarters of the British Empire had to be made grand, and it was, and now is becoming so again. At last, there has been money in the till to do the job. The Indian economic miracle was in full swing.

Singh and his Congress government did a good job with redistribution, pushing money to work programs and social services for the poor. Much gets skimmed by a corrupt bureaucracy, but some at least does what it is meant to do. The middle class is rapidly expanding in cities such as Kolkata—so are the numbers of a very rich, over-pampered, often ignorant and insensitive elite. In Mumbai they are building skyscrapers. "Why don't the poor in the shanty towns buy one of these new high-rise flats?" a famous theatre director asked me at a roof party in Kolkata, "instead of spending their money on mobile phones?"

In Kolkata, a low-rise city, which plans to stay that way, at least in the centre, and where the poor do have proper homes, money is being spent on the restoration and rehabilitation of its huge numbers of striking Victorian and Georgian townhouses, some of them very large indeed, to make company offices, expensive shops and flats for the upper middle class.

Kolkata is throbbing with an economic miracle. Its GNP '' grows at over 10% a year. It was slow off the mark, thanks to a Communist government in West Bengal—it governed for 34 years, 1977 to 2011, the longest running democratically elected Communist government in the world—that frowned on private enterprise. But the Communists had their Road to Damascus conversion when the Chief Minister went to China, met Deng Xiaoping and saw the truth of one of his sayings, "It doesn't matter if the cat is black or white as long as it catches mice". Since around 1994 the

Communists have become helter skelter capitalists, seeking investors who have an urge to combine Kolkata's pool of well-educated labour and professionals with their capital. Foreign investment started to pour in. No longer do the educated young people migrate to Mumbai, Delhi or Bangalore. It is widely regarded as the talent hub of India. These days it is the third most productive metro area after Mumbai and Delhi.

The city has transformed thousands of acres of an outlying district into what it calls "The New City". There are row upon row of new skyscrapers, interspersed with large parks, big shopping malls and the offices of every computer company I've ever heard of. This is to be the new Bangalore.

Long a well-educated part of India, West Bengal, and in particular Kolkata, has produced a disproportionate number of India's intellectuals and artists. The other day one of its returning sons and one of its six Nobel Prize winners, the economist Amatya Sen, gave a speech at his alma mater, Presidency College, wondering if the reason for Kolkata's very low crime rate (the lowest of any big city in the world) is because of the depth of its artistic culture. (Others would point to the exceptionally close Bengali family and neighbourhood structure.)

Not just locals but also many Western readers are devouring Bengali novelists like Amitav Ghosh, Amit Chaudhuri, Jhumpa Lahiri, Rana Dasgupta and Kunal Basu. The annual book fair here is the biggest in India. It stretches almost as far as the eye can see, causes immense traffic jams and makes one realize how important books are to hundreds of thousands of people. Besides new works, the tables were stacked with Tagore, his poems, his songs, his plays and the scores of the writers who have written about him. He is to West Bengal what Shakespeare is to us and there isn't hardly an evening when one of his works isn't being performed.

Theatre culture is thriving. So is film. The greatest Indian film maker of the twentieth century, the late Satyajit Ray, lived in the city. So today does Buddhadeb Dasgupta, a poet, a film maker and an icon for film aficionados. All his films are shot locally. "When

I'm away I can't write" he told me. "I'm now writing a script for my next film. I have to be in Calcutta. I have to have that love of the people, the smell, see the trams, the double deckers and the pot holed streets, the classical charm of the old buildings. If one can absorb the first shock of arrival — the smells, the poverty, then you discover the wonder of the city. The people here are very loving and caring people. They always have time for you."

After talking to Dasgupta I started asking everyone I met who had grown up in the city if they liked it with a similar intensity. They all seemed to. There is an artist who has his home in my street. I knocked on his door without an appointment and, as is the Bengali custom, was immediately invited in. He has many of his latest works hanging in a big room. I wouldn't say they were particularly good — Bengal does not excel in the plastic arts — but in a few there was a touch of Gaugin. "The city looks crowded and dirty", he said. "But the people who live here are good people, cooperative people. Look at the metro — we were the first city in India to build one [now extended to the airport]. As a people we are so proud of it. You will never see one cigarette butt or piece of wrapping paper on the floor. It is spotless."

Joy Dasgupta, an ex-student friend of a journalist I knew, now working partly in the city and partly in the Himalayas in a development project, disagrees with this view of city harmony. "It's not a communal city. The Muslims — a minority — and the Hindus have separate spaces. 30,000 died at the time of partition. Later there were riots in 1992. But not since then, apart from sporadic riots in 1996. The rioting by Muslims was Muslims who didn't have Bengali as their mother tongue — they came from the north."

He is critical too of the working culture. "When the Communists came to power in state elections 46 years ago they were hostile to the capitalists and encouraged strikes. The strikes are less now that the Communists have gone capitalist. But the early period left a legacy of work shyness which is only now being overcome. The political culture panders to populist notions and the workers don't respect the rule of law or the need for productivity. The buses still have thirty employees for driving and maintaining each bus [a bit of an exaggeration]. Nevertheless, these days people do want to make the state work and build a better life with hard work, but this attitude is still in its infancy. The bureaucracy is a barrier to progress. The local government has to recruit people from the small towns who haven't been infected by the old ideas."

Ranabir Roy-Chaudhary is the editor of a newspaper, "The Bengal Post". (Newspaper readership in India is going up fast and new papers are sprouting all over.) He talks about the dirtiness of the city, despite the streets being cleaned every day. "Attitude is a problem. A man who wouldn't throw anything away on the metro or spit, as soon as he leaves the exit goes back to spitting and littering. Thanks to the Communists the people have the idea of rights but not of duties, and that makes for a lazy workforce. But, to give them their due, the Communists have extended education and organised medical services to nearly all the poor. The lakes and parks are well looked after — they could easily have become crime-ridden places. Today there is much more appreciation of the fine buildings."

Parwez Hafeez, the Bengal editor of The Age, a national paper, talks of the success of the changeover from Marxism to capitalism (although the ex-Chief Minister of West Bengal, Buddhadeb Bhattacharjee, had a picture of Lenin in his office and told me that he is still a Marxist). The city has attracted back educated Bengalis who left for better opportunities in other cities, and also Bengalis from the Diaspora in the United States and the UK. He disagrees with those who say Kolkata is not a cohesive society. "The communal togetherness can't be found in other cities", he says. "People who migrate here from other states talk about the warmth of Kolkata. It's a remarkable melting pot of languages and religion. This is what makes Kolkata a city of joy".

My final stop for interviews was the mayor, Sovan Chatarjee. He had been elected on the ticket of the Trinamool Congress Party, breaking the stranglehold of the Communists. At that time Ms Mamata Banerjee, its leader, was in coalition with the ruling Congress Party and she was the central government's minister for the railways. An unmarried woman who had devoted her life to politics she led her party to a trouncing of the Communists in the state election of 2011. The Communists had overstayed their welcome, accused of ineptitude and corruption. It must be said in their defence that Ms Banerjee's party has many of the same bad characteristics. Ms Banerjee has also played footsie with the Maoists whose insurgency has bedevilled part of West Bengal's rural hinterland. It was widely assumed her party would be lucky to last more than one term. In fact, she won a third one, such is the progress in the economy and the disarray in the Communists' camp. Her most popular success is the introduction of a scheme whereby women under the age of 60 received free basic financial help of 500 rupees — $6 — every month. (1000 for minorities.)

The mayor's interview with me was conducted out of the right side of his mouth whilst he dealt with continuous phone calls out of the left. Everyone seemed to have his number and he answered almost every call. His policies were the down to earth ones: better solid waste management — the sewers were laid down by the British — the widening and maintenance of the potholed roads and, for the poorer areas, a twenty-four-hour water supply. Garbage removal is the number one issue, he says. After that comes pollution which is severe. He became eloquent when talking about the need to beautify the city. The last Communist government knocked down many of the abandoned factories along the Ganges and made a long park along its shore. He wants more of this. "Then we can get tourists", he claimed. "But first we have to make the city green."

The British in fact bequeathed a very green city, planting trees on every street which have now matured into 15-metre-high leafy shade. Talking of the British, their legacy in India is profound and nowhere more so than in Kolkata — the quality of the best schools and universities; the perfect colloquial English spoken by the well-educated, and even their sense of humour and irony; the style and interests of middle class life; the standard and reach of a free, questioning, press; the introduction of parliamentary government all the way down to small villages; the use of English law, replacing the haphazard forms that existed before; the concept of economic development rather than centuries of inertia; and, not least, the railways, now being modernised in West Bengal and all over at a hectic rate, with money being spent to improve the whole system, not concentrating on a few high speed TGV-type trains as they are in China. Indeed India—frugal Kolkata and West Bengal in particular—is not known for white elephants and spreads its development progress much wider than China where it is concentrated on its eastern and southern coasts. The Indian way fits in with the European and North American way much more than the Chinese.

This is why for two decades I have maintained that before too long India will overtake China. And why I tend to go along with the mantra of some of my Kolkata friends and acquaintances that we will live to see the city taking its place beside Bangkok, Mumbai, Shanghai and Jakarta as one of the world's up and coming great cities—and with far more charm than any of them.

Chapter 11
The coming death of Jimmy Carter

"The lives of all politicians end in failure". So said Enoch Powell, a maverick former cabinet minister in the British government.

Of recent US presidents Jimmy Carter has not been alone in being considered "a failure". Think of Lyndon Johnson (Vietnam war). George W. Bush (Iraq war). Bill Clinton (Monica Lewinsky and a wasted last term). George H.W. Bush (messing up the economy and laying the foundation along with Clinton for the great economic crash of 2007). Ronald Reagan (missing the chance with Soviet president Mikhail Gorbachev to create the nuclear-free world that he offered). Richard Nixon (Firing up the Vietnam War and having to resign in disgrace). Then there was Barack Obama who missed the opportunity to forge a great rapprochement with Russia. Then there was Joe Biden who repeated Johnson's deadly mix—progressive on domestic policy and warlike and massively deceptive when it came to dealing with Russia and fighting a proxy war. As for Donald Trump...........

Back to Jimmy Carter

I had a tangential responsibility for his election. I went to interview him in Atlanta when he was governor of Georgia. I spent the best part of the afternoon and early evening with him—being offered only a coke for dinner!

He took me into his bedroom to see his small library of books. He plucked down a copy of a sort of biography cum manifesto he had written. "I'm a bit short of copies", he said. "Can you mail it back once you have read it?" I did. I was foolish not to have asked him to autograph it since shortly after, unexpectedly, he won the fight to become president.

I also put my foot in it. I am a good friend of Andrew Young, who was Martin Luther King's chief of staff. We got to know each other when I worked on the staff of Dr King and his "End the Slums" campaign in Chicago. Young was also from Atlanta. He was then a congressman and later Carter appointed him Ambassador to the UN.

I told Carter about our friendship. Carter asked, "What does he think of me?" I replied, "Not much".

At a reception shortly after Carter accosted Young about this remark which led to Young explaining why he felt like that. They had a number of meetings after that cleared the air. Young was an important player in national politics.

Soon after Carter announced he was going to run for president. Young agreed to join his team. According to Carter, Young won the election for him by getting out the black southern vote. The new president repeated it many times. Shortly after Carter had won I visited Young and he said, laughing, "Look what you have done with your big mouth—elected the president of the United States"!

Carter gave Young a carte blanche to run America's African policy, not least the effort to end white rule in Rhodesia and South Africa. Carter was persuaded by Young to ask Congress to introduce tight economic sanctions against South Africa.

In a policy forged by Zbigniew Brzezinski, the president's national security advisor, who I interviewed at length many times, the US secretly shipped modern weapons, including the deadly Stinger missiles, to support the successful effort by the Afghanis to drive the army of the Soviet Union out of Afghanistan.

If that was a victory what followed was not. It led to civil war, with the best armed faction, the Taliban, winning out. Later they gave a home and base to Al Qaeda which added Saudi Arabian arms and money to build up its strength. From here Al Qaeda prepared for 9/11.

The US under George W. Bush decided because of 9/11 to bomb Afghanistan in an attempt to squash Al-Qaeda. They succeeded although Al-Qaeda, having moved to Pakistan, morphed into ISIS.

The US and NATO went on fighting the Taliban until three when they finally withdrew in August of 2021, defeated. That was a living out of Carter's legacy. The whole effort by seven successive presidents beginning with Carter was a cause for disgrace.

But, fortunately, there is far more to Carter than that.

Carter, a highly religious man who taught in his local Sunday school whenever he could get home, felt that God had created the US in part "to set an example for the rest of the world". Human rights was to be the centre piece of his foreign policy, he kept saying. In practice it wasn't so straightforward. As Hodding Carter, the State Department's spokesman at that time once observed, his human rights policy was "ambiguous, ambivalent and ambidextrous". Hodding Carter's wife, Patricia Derian, who was the assistant secretary for human rights, was often frustrated by the lack of support from her superiors.

Carter's new policy was most effective in the Western hemisphere. After he was defeated for a second term, he visited Argentina and was swamped by crowds who thanked him for helping undermine the military regime which had imprisoned and tortured a wide range of opposition activists. The Catholic Church in Argentina, of which the present pope was an important member, was largely silent, unlike its counterparts in Chile and Brazil where there were also repressive military regimes. Thus, the role that Carter played was an unprecedentedly successful, non-violent, intervention. It brought results. The regime was weakened and eventually toppled. A similar impact was made in several other Latin American countries. Arms sales were cut off and a number of countries were economically squeezed.

Carter did raise human rights to a new level of political potency. Certainly in Latin America, but also in Indonesia, India, Myanmar, East Timor and South Korea, he emboldened religious, labour and liberal groups to be more openly critical of their regimes. Carter told the South Korean military regime that he would pull out all US troops if they executed Kim Dae-jung, the opposition leader, who went on to become president.

More than this, Carter's human rights crusade provided both then and today a yardstick against which the foreign policy of Western nations came to be judged, even when Carter partly turned his back on his earlier commitment.

One serious flaw was Carter's obsession with defeating communism in the Soviet Union. He mislaid his sense of even-handedness. Even in his final speech at the Democratic Party Convention he singled out the USSR as a human rights pariah while giving no mention of the rest of the world.

When the Soviet Union invaded Afghanistan to impose a Marxist regime it spurred Carter to orientate the US towards China. Carter, who had vowed during his campaign for the presidency he wouldn't "ass-kiss" the Chinese, paid no heed to the jailing of Democracy Wall activists in 1979. Carter was intent on concluding the formal normalization of relations with China. Carter looked the other way when the important Chinese dissident Wei Jingsheng was sentenced to fifteen years' imprisonment. Yet at more or less the same time Carter was lambasting Moscow for sending Soviet dissident Anatol Sharansky to prison.

Carter's worst bit of dual thinking — you can call it hypocrisy — was his policy towards Cambodia. When the US withdrew from Vietnam, Cambodia under its villainous leader Pol Pot became not just a thorn in the flesh of Vietnam, it killed an estimated 1.7 million of its own people in a massive genocide — the so-called "Killing Fields", (the title of a superb movie). In 1978 Carter declared Cambodia "the worst violator of human rights in the world".

But Carter anxious not to cross China which he was wooing said little more. China was Pol Pot's friend. "I encouraged the Chinese to support Pol Pot," Zbigniew Brzezinski, told the New York Times. He was wedded to the old Henry Kissinger formula of "playing the China card" against the Soviet Union.

As Jonathan Alter has written in Foreign Policy magazine, "it got worse". He explained: "The US supported Pol Pot's claim to the Cambodian seat in the United Nations. Pol Pot's flag flew outside the UN building. All the European nations, except Sweden, joined the US in its recognition of the Pol Pot government".

Many diplomatic and journalistic observers have argued that China would not have broken off its rapprochement with the US if Carter had decided not to go along with supporting the Pol Pot government. China had too much at stake with the US to allow a tail to wag the dog. Indeed, when the Vietnamese finally toppled Pol Pot, China stood by.

Carter' legacy *is* mixed. His supporters say that his compromises were matched by his successes, particular in the USSR. Victor Havel, the dissident playwright who later became the president of the Czech Republic, said that not only did Carter inspire him in prison, he also undermined the "self-confidence" of the Soviet bloc. The self-confidence of Eastern Europe's human rights organizations did grow.

The former Soviet ambassador to Washington, Anatoly Dobrynin, wrote in his memoirs that Carter's human rights policies "played a significant role" in the Soviet Union, loosening its grip at home and in Eastern Europe. Once liberalization was under way, Dobrynin concluded, it couldn't be controlled.

The image of the US as an upholder of human rights is badly tarnished after the tenure of George W. Bush and Donald Trump. There are many faults to be remedied at home before other countries will take the US as seriously as they used to. True, thanks to Carter's convictions, human rights does run through the bloodstream of the Democratic Party. But before getting caught up in challenging and criticizing others as he does regularly, the present president, Joe Biden, should put his own American house in order. At home the list of constant human rights abuses is a long one. American democracy is not in a healthy state.

Carter's life is not ending in failure. Despite his mistakes in Afghanistan and vis a vis the Soviet Union, we have much to thank him for compared with other presidents.

Chapter 12
My Search for the Swedish Soul

An examination of the Swedish soul must begin, I'm afraid, with sex. Not Volvo, not IKEA, not Alfa Laval nor H&M. Not Strindberg nor Dagerman nor even Astrid Lindgren and Pippi Longstocking. Not the welfare state, not income equality nor criminal justice. Not the Lutheran Church nor collective bargaining. Not the Vikings, nor 200 years without war. It's that three letter word — and the half-myth about Swedish promiscuity — that is our starting point.

The town I live in, Lund, across the bridge from Copenhagen, hosts not only Scandinavia's oldest university and cathedral, it is full of high-tech companies including some of the ones mentioned above and many computer technology, biotech and pharmaceutical start-ups. It is where I have lived for the last seventeen years. It hosts thousands of students and the weekends are notoriously wild. But the students are bright and after I've given a lecture which I do occasionally I like to take those who want to out for a drink.

Inevitably, the subject turns to sex and marriage. I'll never forget asking one group what they thought of marriage in a country where most educated young people (and half go to university) don't get married or bear children until they are well over 30. A young woman gave me a thoughtful answer and so I asked her, "What are you looking for in a husband?" Without batting an eye or pausing for thought, she answered: "Three things. One, he must be good in bed. Two, he must be a good father. Three, when we divorce, he mustn't be bitter."

I've tried this story out on all sorts of Swedes and all ages, and they laugh a bit self-consciously and nod and say, "That's true," or "I'm afraid so." But if my student had been a little fairer she would have added that most Swedish men push the pram, do the nappies, get up in the night to feed the baby and help clean the house. Many, too, take at least six months off to look after the baby while the woman goes back to work.

Young students I know well, even though they are in a happy and what they call "permanent relationship" will say that they have no intention of getting married. Children, yes, but not until they are at least 35. Today's 35s still get married, although usually after the children are born. My generation universally did marry. But all three generations and a good part of the one before believe you should have all the sex you can reasonably find before marriage. Mind you, this generation is different in that it doesn't mate for love but for pleasure. The students here are big on one-night stands with people they barely know. (Their mothers and fathers can be rather appalled.)

Women in this society hold their heads very high. Alexandra von Schwerin, a journalist and entrepreneur, explained it to me as she sees it: "They have been used to being independent since Viking times when the men went away for years in their long boats. Women began to be educated in large numbers at the beginning of the 20th century and equality has been pushed hard ever since. The glass ceiling in the business world still remains almost impenetrable for top positions, but in all the professions women have equal pay and authority. All women work. Women have been working for four generations now. My great-grandmother worked. And all working parents have access to a municipal run crèche for their children, even for those only a year old."

In short, a woman is almost as free as a man. Divorce is nothing to fear. The money and house will be divided equally without the need for an expensive divorce lawyer. Most divorced women sail happily along with no great financial worries, with a caring state ready to prop them up if something gives way.

So where did this attitude to sex and marriage come from? When I was a student, we used to be told that it was the films of Ingmar Bergman, as well as the first feature film on general release to show sexual intercourse on screen — I am Curious, Yellow — which starred the late prime minister, Olof Palme, talking about sex. But in truth, this sexual liberation has roots that go much further back.

I asked the literary critic and secretary of the Nobel literature prize committee Horace Engdahl, about this. His answer was: "Urbanisation came late in Sweden, and consequently the influence of the middle class with its strict norms of sexual behaviour has been limited. In the countryside, boys and girls were traditionally allowed to make each other's acquaintance, to 'woo for the night' as long as they showed responsibility in avoiding or taking care of the consequences. Virginity has never been a big thing in Sweden."

The role of the countryside explains all manner of things. Swedes are entwined with it. In the summer very few go abroad, apart from young backpackers seeking adventure. Eighty per cent of the people want to be in their little red wooden summer house, preferably by a lake or the sea. (The poor have caravans.) Many summers are full of rain, but the memories stretching way back to childhood keep them coming back — marvellous warm summers with cousins pouring in to taste the fresh caught crayfish and to frisk in the unpolluted water. A quick look at the cosy, blossom filled paintings of Carl Larsson puts you right in the picture. The idyll can be true.

Historically, the aristocracy was spread thin in the countryside and there was no large and powerful rural upper or even middle class that wanted to enclose the peasants' land and push them out to work in the dark satanic mills. Hence the yeoman peasants ruled the countryside, and this is the origin of the near-classless society of modern Sweden. It is also, as Prime Minister Fredrick Reinfeldt explained to me, why war has been out of favour in Sweden for over 200 years. "In the 18th and 17th centuries the idea of Sweden as a military superpower was solely the idea of the king. There was a handshake between royalty and the peasants. But eventually the peasants began to think that war and campaigning all over Europe, as far as Russia, was too heavy a burden. Because the peasants owned their own land they were autonomous. And so they rejected war, at a time when royalty was going through a weakened period after 1814."

In the 18th century Swedish prowess on the battlefield made it a European superpower. But the Napoleonic wars were its undoing: Sweden experienced its greatest ever defeat, losing Finland, a third of Sweden's territory and a quarter of its population, to the Russia of Tsar Alexander I. Sweden's generals still planned for war after that—and did right through to the Cold War when, although officially neutral, they were clearly part of the western alliance's military infrastructure, even if the electorate was not allowed to know it. But, on the face of things, Sweden renounced wars of aggression in 1814. From then on peace was perceived as Swedish and wars as European. Swedes today like to think, as members of the EU, that the Swedish peace has now been Europeanised. All this has unexpectedly (at least for most Swedes) been overturned by the Russian invasion of Ukraine.

In the Second World War Sweden did make a Faustian pact with Hitler that in return for its neutrality it would allow the transit of iron ore to Germany's industrial war machine. Following the end of the war Sweden developed a guilty conscience over its failure to have done so little to help its Nordic neighbours. However, it did bask in Jewish praise for having cooperated with the Danish resistance and given refuge to so many fleeing Jews. And ever since the war it has transformed its guilty conscience by becoming the world's conscience over matters of third world development, helping to end apartheid in South Africa (it was the only western nation to give significant funds to the African National Congress), opposing the war in Vietnam and giving shelter to American deserters, cancelling its well-advanced effort to build its own nuclear bomb and, not least, being a vigorous and fairly consistent champion of human rights (although it spoiled its reputation by being party to President Bush's policy of rendition).

Lack of war is a major reason for Sweden's remarkable economic advance. In a matter of 100 years it moved from being one of the poorest parts of Europe with a massive exodus of near-starving people to America to being one of the two richest countries in Europe (the other was Switzerland.) It has produced more world-class industrial giants than any other country of its size. (At 10.5 million, its population is less than that of the state of Michigan.)

While other European countries were struggling to rebuild themselves at the end of the Second World War, Sweden was striding ahead. Perhaps inevitably it looked to America for inspiration which led to such un-European things as straight roads, old wooden towns knocked down to be replaced by ugly concrete flats—lending them a rather sterile ambiance which is not helped by the almost total absence of pubs and cafes (although lately immigrants have brought in pizza and kebab restaurants). Still, the countryside, masses of it, remains gorgeously undisturbed, and in summer appears like another France.

Maybe Sweden became too comfortable, too spoiled and resting on the laurels of its ubiquitous welfare state. Whatever the reason, in the 1970s and 1980s it lost its economic edge. In 1992 a number of its banks crashed and had to be dramatically saved by the right-wing government of Carl Bildt. Sweden's success in nationalising the banks for a few years, restoring them to health and then privatising them at a handsome profit, is regarded as a model for crisis-torn countries today. (Nationalised industries have long been anathema—with a few exceptions—in this otherwise socialist state. Sweden, long before Thatcherism took hold, privatised its railways.)

More recently, though, Sweden has become one of the leading internet technology countries. Under Prime Minister Goran Persson (1996-2006) the country's growth rate per head was consistently the highest in the western world and its unemployment one of the lowest. During the Great Depression that started in 2011 Sweden bucked the German-led European consensus on austerity and continued with its Keynesian economics. Thus it had a better growth rate than any other EU country bar Poland. This economic success has made the pursuit of equality and social wellbeing relatively easy. Nevertheless, the roots of the pursuit of equality in Sweden go deeper.

When I asked my tenant, Karin Stalhammar—a clever, well read, medical student, aged 22—where this equality came from she replied, "We learned it just by growing up here. It has gone into our bloodstream." A trade union official I talked to, Eva Palsoon, echoed this: "I sometimes think we are born with it." Sophia Nerbrand, editor of the intellectual magazine, Neo, argues that it is "because Sweden never had feudalism. Everyone had their own land. We inherited the ethos of the village to work collectively." The recent Prime Minister Fredrick Reinfeldt explained it to me thus: "We have a deeply held feeling we can afford it. The Swedish electorate don't just look at their own wallet. They do want to see poorer people better off."

Yet in spite of this, the rich in Sweden do stay rich. I asked one friend, Rikard Uddenberg, a prosperous businessman, how this was. "The tax system was very harsh 30 years ago. If you had a good idea it was difficult to expand. But there have been many changes since then, starting with Olof Palme's government and gathering speed since then. Now Sweden's corporate tax is lower than many other countries."

He admits that when he grew up the prevailing ethos among the rich was to secretly put their money in Liechtenstein. "That's how I thought too." But he had had a road to Damascus event in his life. Four years ago his first born baby was diagnosed with a dangerous heart ailment. She was treated by a Libyan doctor in one of the world's top children's heart clinics in Sweden and has now recovered, a happy little girl. "Then I realised what went on inside the system I had rather derided. I saw what the tax system did with our money and how effective it was. The treatment did not cost me a krona. More than anything this changed my attitude."

Even the current, conservative Swedish prime ministers don't want to change this attitude or these facts. "We are not building a separate system. We just want better results, so people can grow," Reinfeldt told me.

Then Reinfeldt was leading the four conservative parties who formed the government to reform some of the deeply held attitudes of Swedish society. "What we are is anti-conformity. We have opened up the schools and health services to competition and worked to end the many monopolies in our society." The propensity towards conformity bugs both Reinfeldt and many of the foreigners who work or study here. When I said that I find the Swedes are the Japanese of Europe, he nodded his head in agreement.

Apart from a well-travelled elite, the majority of people look down on those who buck the Swedish lifestyle trend—those who are a day late at the end of every month with paying their bills, those who cross the street before the light turns green even if no traffic is coming, those who miss a meeting of the committee of tenants that supervise their block of flats, those who don't do immediately what the committee has told them to do. (The penalties are severe—as I found out. You can be thrown onto the street for disobeying, even though you own your flat). Swedes just about can bring themselves to vote for different parties. But when it comes to big issues they usually follow the Stockholm elite's consensus. Very rarely is there a furious debate in parliament or the courtroom. People prefer to agree than disagree. Still the decision this year, after nearly 200 years of avoiding military entanglements, the government decided to join NATO shattered some shibboleths about Sweden. Conservative politicians and media succeeded in whipping up opinion to believe "the Russians were coming", even though they never came during the Second World War or the Cold War. The government shunned calling for a referendum, although for big issues the Swedes usually do have referenda. The government realized it would lose.

Swedes tell you that there is pressure in society not to raise your head too far above the parapet. One shouldn't push too hard to get ahead, to ask too demandingly for a salary increase, to engage in conspicuous consumption, to build too big a house or to own too posh a car or dress in a fancy or even stylish way. The very well-cut business suit or skirt and jacket, much less the bejewelled theatre, concert or partygoer are not welcomed. Still, on rare occasions, the Swedes can laugh at themselves (although humour is more often verging on the slapstick than clever or ironic). Pippi Longstocking, for example, is everything Swedes are not—the way she dressed, her abhorrence of convention, even bringing her pet horse to live in her house—but they love her.

The Swedes are constantly debating education—partly because the 1960s batch of teachers, now rather senior, have such a laid-back attitude and the pupils no longer behave very well. (They have no idea how good the children are compared to their British counterparts.) Tove Klette, leader of the ruling Folk Party in Lund's town hall, worries that in today's world "we need the crème de la crème to create a more competitive system. We must start with the schools. We must copy Finland which comes top of the world's league table in education. We have to raise the status and the respect given to teachers. We need teachers with PhDs, as in Finland, and let them, when not teaching, do research. We need streaming and fast tracking." There are only a handful of what we would call fee-paying public schools in the whole of Sweden. The overwhelming majority of schools are comprehensives, and do well on the international league tables, better than Britain, France or Germany, and they are often as good as Britain's top public schools. And a new batch of private schools, launched by the government of Carl Bildt a decade ago, are as well financially supported by the government as are state schools. A kind of voucher system exists for all children and educational practice in Sweden is constantly changing and being improved.

Yet even Klette's counterpart, the Social Democrat leader Anders Almgren concedes that with the educational and welfare state as it is today, "We are in danger of thinking that it is part of natural science and can't be changed. We should never get too tolerant of abuse of the system, or become naive. We should never allow people to abuse the welfare state—this then becomes an excuse for discarding the fundamentals of the Swedish model."

At the same time he is worried that the more rigorous and competitive policies of the government are undermining Sweden's sense of equality in education and health. "The private health clinics cream off the easy, money making, cases and leave the difficult ones to the national health service. And in the small towns a private school can rob the sole state school of its best pupils."

The universities need a shake-up too. Now that the OECD is publishing annual league tables for European universities they can see how well or poorly they are doing. Lund and Uppsala (often referred to wrongly as the Oxbridge of Sweden) are down in the mid-forties. Copenhagen, a few kilometres away, is in the first ten. Per Eriksson, the vice-chancellor of Lund University, says they are planning changes—including a late attempt to recruit well-paid foreign professors to replace some of the ingrown Swedish ones and ordering lecturing for all masters' degrees to be in English. One advantage of Swedish universities, though, is that there are no fees, which is very helpful to a freelance writer like me with a daughter and is why foreign students flock here—a very good investment for Sweden.

One thing one can say with little debate is that Swedish society is a post-religious one. But although its attachment to Lutheranism has died, its social mores still reflect its heritage. As Nietzsche once wrote, "Those who have abandoned God cling much harder to their moral beliefs." Reinfeldt echoes the sentiment. "Without the link to God anymore, the basic ideas stayed on."

Three examples of this stand out: drugs, alcohol and prostitution. There is very little prostitution. It's always been penalised, but now the penalties fall mainly on the customer rather than the prostitute. Which man wants to see his name in the papers? Likewise, there has long been a tough attitude to drugs. Children at school are gently brainwashed on the subject—although my daughter when 16 was prepared in a school debate (by her own will) to echo her father's point, that legalisation would reduce the problem. The teacher appeared not to welcome her intervention. How is it that Sweden has successfully kept drugs out to a greater extent than many other countries? Once again Swedish conformism provides a good part of the answer.

Alcohol is a more divisive issue. In the 19th century Sweden had a vodka problem. Prohibition came in and did have a dramatic effect on consumption, despite the forest stills. Later in the early 20th century the government eased up and allowed state-owned shops to sell very high-priced alcohol. Certainly, price is a deterrent, although Goran Persson, when prime minister, complained to me that EU policies on free trade were eating away at high prices and thus increasing alcohol drinking in Sweden. (Swedes rarely drink in moderation each day of the week; their idea of fun is to over-drink at the weekend.)

Sweden has long been seen as a cultural backwater in Europe. Only in the last 100 years, as transport and trade have improved, did Sweden plug into the rest of Europe. Go back to the 18th century, much less the 16th, there is no Shakespeare, no Milton, no Jane Austen or, to compare it with Russia, no Tolstoy, Dostoyevsky, or Chekhov. Similarly, there have been no truly great artists, composers, or philosophers. (Denmark has had Kierkegaard, Norway Grieg, and Finland Sibelius.) However, it has produced three important film makers: Bergman, Bo Winderberg and Jan Troell whose latest film, Everlasting Moments, received much acclaim.

Few students read much literature and Swedish newspapers, by the standards of Europe and even its neighbour, little Denmark, are second rate. For Swedes, young and old, the world is a faraway place about which they know little. (Nevertheless, almost paradoxically, they are the most generous of all peoples in helping poorer nations.)

When I asked Horace Engdahl about all this he replied somewhat defensively: "High culture is every bit as important as it is in Germany, France or Britain, and has a comparative amplitude, if you consider the relative size of these nations. [Sweden's population is around one seventh of Britain's.] More people watch theatre than football. The same thing goes for opera, which has been experiencing an upsurge. More books are sold and read than ever before in history. My sons know more about opera and contemporary art than I did in school and read philosophy."

I give Engdahl his due. "The question about the extent of high culture," I said diplomatically, "remains an open one."

But, perhaps most important of all, Swedes are happy and almost as family orientated as the Italians. One survey says they are the happiest nation in the world, despite their taciturnity, their love of privacy and their lack of hospitality to strangers. Some disagree — according to Sibylla Weigert, who is a senior architect with IKEA, "Swedes are very 'I' orientated. Before I had children and we had a lot of girlie get-togethers a common line of conversation was how can I get my husband to see how important I am."

But Christina Ramberg, a top commercial lawyer from Gothenburg and someone who always votes right, was the most articulate of all the people I talked to. She argued that, "Sweden is a wonderful place for women and children. Swedes are more economically productive than anyone else because at work we work. We work very hard, even without the boss being on our backs. That's why we have a high national income and can take the longest holidays of any industrialised nation. Moreover, we don't see the state as an opponent, but as a friend. I find it hard, having travelled and worked all over the world, to come up with any negatives about Sweden."

No negatives? Well, a few. Pushed by my homesick Swedish wife I arrived from living in sunny Spain right by the sea and almost immediately went into depression. (See chapter 1.) The weather was grey and forbidding, and the people similar. I found it difficult to make friends or to make an entry into university life. I was isolated. I sat by myself for weeks on end in a dungeon of a cafe writing a book. Perhaps, not surprisingly, my 17 year-long marriage ended in divorce, although my daughter, 34, keeps me here. (And now Jeany's Alzheimer's.) After six years I began to find my feet. These days I have a small batch of friends, some Swedish. But it's been a long journey and I know that a majority of foreigners who are brought here by their Swedish partners have not dissimilar difficult experiences. But in fairness, I would conclude that Sweden is not at all bad — given how the rest of world is.

Chapter 13
A Political Paul

I went to school with Paul McCartney in Liverpool over 60 years ago, and we have remained friends, albeit distant, ever since. He launched at our old school, the Liverpool Institute, the publication of my book," Like Water On Stone — The Story Of Amnesty International" (Penguin 2010). I got the ball rolling, and made the introduction on stage, for a performance in February 2017 of his marvellous first classical piece, the Liverpool Oratorio, in the magnificent and important Frankfurt Opera House. Jeany also sang the female lead in a dramatized version of the piece in a pretty experimental theatre in a Frankfurt park.

I joined the school a few years after most of the boys in my class — my parents moved from Manchester to Liverpool. Alan Durband, our form master, asked Paul to make me feel at home. And he did just that. It was an act of kindness I remembered long after. I knew how boys could be.

At the first lunch break he invited me to walk to the corner street where stood — and still does — a small sweet and cigarette shop. He bought me an ice lolly while we talked about where I had come from and how I'd arrived at the school. He asked me if I liked cricket and I told him that I did a lot but wasn't great at it. "That's good, he said with a laugh, "Let's go back to the yard and we'll play" So we did with a tennis ball and a dozen other boys, a practice we kept up all through the summer term. I got no hint of his musical interests until O levels were over and we were studying for A levels, the university entrance exams. I was rehearsing a play and in the next-door classroom Paul and George were practising. It was very early days and they were a bit screechy and I had to go to their room and ask them to keep the decibels down whilst we were mastering our lines.

The Liverpool Institute High School for Boys was then the city's top state grammar school, drawing some middle and middle upper class but, in the main, the brightest of the working class and lower middle class — one of our old boys, Charles Glover Barkla, won the Nobel Prize for physics. The Institute was the choir school of Liverpool cathedral. Paul auditioned for the choir but didn't get in — apparently the music teacher didn't think he was good enough. Another Beatle, George Harrison, was in the year below Paul. (John Lennon and Ringo Starr were educated elsewhere in the city — at Quarry Bank grammar school and Dingles secondary modern respectively.) The Liverpool Institute closed in 1985. Eleven years later, Paul opened the Liverpool Institute for Performing Arts, a famed academy for aspiring artists, on the site.

Paul is not known for his political views — John was always thought of as the political Beatle. But having been a political journalist for most of my life I wanted to talk to Paul about, among other things, the great political events of our lifetimes. I wanted it to be a casual conversation, like two old men (Ha! Ha!) sitting on a bench reminiscing about school days and some of the things that have happened since.

JONATHAN POWER: In different ways, me as a journalist you as a rock star, we have both had a ringside seat on the last 50 years — the 1960s, Vietnam, Nixon, Thatcher, Blair, the end of the cold war, Iraq and so on. But let's start with the Second World War. In your classical work of 17 years ago, the Liverpool Oratorio, you included a lot of wartime memories.

PAUL McCARTNEY: Yes. My dad had a hearing defect and couldn't join the army, so he was in the fire service which was pretty hazardous because Liverpool was bombed heavily. He was quite a jovial guy and didn't talk about it much himself. But I did know about incendiary bombs and so on. And I remember sirens; I was born in 1942. I remember there being a kind of gung-ho spirit about the war. Later on during our teenage years, my first reaction was to say I'm a pacifist. But then I also knew that if we had been invaded I would have defended my country, my family — the animal instinct in me would have taken over. I have experienced it in minor ways on my farm when, for example, a ram butted one of the kids and I attacked him back. The animal in me said, "How bloody dare you! Right, mate!" and I had a go at him.

POWER: The Second World War is seen by most people as a good war. But the First World War is generally regarded as a stupid mistake — and one that led to most of the horrors of the 20th century. Most wars, with good sense, can be avoided. We all know Iraq could have been avoided. I have argued so could the Second World War…

McCARTNEY: There was a very strong feeling after 9/11 that America had to do something. But I always felt that Bush struck out at the wrong boy in the playground… It could have been avoided, yes.

POWER: I remember reading that your blood was up after 9/11 and that — because of your father — you identified with the firemen who risked their lives at the World Trade Centre, but looking back, do you think you allowed your passion to overrun?

McCARTNEY: Definitely, yes. I think everyone did. I was in New York at the time. I was just taking off at exactly 8.50am and it was one of those memorable announcements from the captain: "Those of you on the right-hand side of the aircraft will notice there has been an accident and this has delayed our take-off." I assumed it had been a runaway plane, as happened once before when someone had a heart attack at the controls. I just thought, "Oh God, it's gone into the Twin Towers and they are both on fire."

Being there, the worry then was "When is the next attack coming?" It was not just fear, it was more "How organised are these people? Are they going to poison the water?" There was a mood to be exploited. I have become quite cynical about how some of these recent wars have been started. Georgia is another example: I had been due to play a concert there in September. I had done a concert in Ukraine and afterwards I met the President of Georgia, Mikhail Saakashvili, at a little lunch party in Kiev given by the promoter. He invited us to go to Georgia to play and I was happy to do that. I like reaching out, particularly to the eastern bloc. They love these concerts; it symbolises freedom for them. I had done Moscow, St Petersburg and, as I say, Kiev. But then I was on holiday in early August and I picked up a New York Times, looked at it and went "my God, what's going on here?" I rang my promoters and they said, "No, the Georgia concert is off."

Then a bit later I was talking to people and I suddenly go click in my mind — I am not normally one for conspiracy theories, but we were in the middle of the presidential election. It was McCain, and Obama, Hillary was out of the running, and I did think "conspiracy theory — you know the Skull and Bones club that Bush was part of at Yale. What do those guys do in a secret society? What do they cook up? I thought, faced with a situation in which McCain looks as if he is losing, they might just say to Saakashvili, "Look you have a couple of regions up there that are playing up, why not do something about this? Why not tick them off and if you need military help we are right behind you, we will help you out." Could an offer like that have been made?

POWER: I don't think it works quite like that. After all, Condoleezza Rice went out to Georgia a month before, and said, "Do not provoke Russia." And Bush was right behind her. However, I think there was also a backroom going on, certainly there were neo-conservative, pro-McCain people, who wanted to take a harder line with the new Russia. And so Saakashvili was getting the official red light but he was also being told at the same time by very influential Americans, "If you do it, Bush will have no choice but to support you." I think that is how it works.

McCARTNEY: Yes, that sounds more likely. But the headline remains: wars can be manufactured, particularly when an economy is ailing.

POWER: When we first knew each other at school I remember making a passionate speech in the debating society, and someone stood up after me and said, "Now I have seen my first angry

186

young man." What were your memories of the politics of that time?

McCARTNEY: My memories would be more musical, more to do with reaching out through music. I remember the end of term, bringing my guitar in, the only day you were allowed to—and standing on the desk of the history teacher Cliff Edge, a particularly nice teacher, and singing Long Tall Sally. I remember George [Harrison] bringing his guitar in too. The reaction you got from all the boys "Yeah! Wow! This is great"—I guess it made an impression and made me think yes, I should do more of this.

POWER: I remember that day! But we were also in a very academic school and we were in the fast stream up to O-levels, four years, not five like everybody else, we were being pressured to look at university. When did you decide to break with that?

McCARTNEY: It is funny; one of the things I love about life is that it often just takes over. You can make great plans, but fate steps in. In my case, I like the way that mistakes sometimes turn out to be the opposite. So I remember hanging around in the classroom one lunchtime and seeing all the guys in my sixth-form class working away at stuff and I said, "What are you doing?" and they said, "Writing to universities" and I had not the slightest clue that you had to do that. Nobody had told me. My mum and dad did not know; dad had been a cotton salesman.

POWER: But the teachers told us all how to do it.

McCARTNEY: Yes, but "McCartney, you never listen!" It was always in my end of term report: "If only he would pay more attention he would do well." I was dreaming. It was considered a crime, but for an artist it is not. In fact, it's a good thing. It's what we do. Fate blocked off the university route—because I didn't know the address of any university or what to say on the form, I think I sent something to a couple of colleges saying more or less "Dear Sir, Let me in."

POWER: Come on, you weren't that stupid! You were one of the brightest boys in our class. You like to make out you were the bad one, but you weren't. Anyway, let's talk about the great cultural upheaval of the 1960s. I think 1968 is overrated; it was the culmination of something earlier – perhaps starting in 1955 when Rosa Parks refused to give up her seat on the bus in Montgomery and this preacher from a small black church emerged from the shadows, Martin Luther King. There was a lot going on before Paris.

McCARTNEY: That's right, I think a lot of the seeds were sown much earlier. But the generation before us had been brought up to toe the line: "Ours is not to reason why; ours is but to do and die." But it became much easier for us to question things. I remember a lady coming to give a talk at the school about her experiences in Rhodesia, as it was then known. It was real colonial talk: "Oh, we have a boy to do that for us" and so on. I remember being annoyed, even though I was just in my early teens, and I asked a question, challenging her attitude. She said, "Oh no, no, no. That is how it is."
And I remember an auntie of mine, who had been lifted over a wall to see a black man when she was a kid because it was so rare, had this same attitude. She said, "No, you can't give them independence, they wouldn't know what to do with it." My reaction was "You must, you have to. We stole it, now we have to give it back."

POWER: In the 2007 film Across the Universe the director weaves a love story around Beatles music and, like quite a few other people, she seems to be saying that you somehow encapsulated this mood of the 1960s – you formed in 1960 after all – and you transmitted it like nobody else had been able to transmit it. Do you think that is true?

McCARTNEY: Maybe. But the nice thing about it was that we didn't do it consciously. We sort of stumbled into things. For instance, Vietnam. Just when we were getting to be well-known someone said to me, "Bertrand Russell is living not far from here in Chelsea why don't you go and see him?" and so I just took a taxi down there and knocked on the door. There was an American guy who was helping him and he came to the door and I said, "I'd like to meet Mr Russell, if possible." I waited a little and then met the great man and he was fabulous. He told me about the Vietnam war—most of us didn't know about it, it wasn't yet in the papers—and also that it was a very bad war. I remember going back to the studio either that evening or the next day and telling the guys, particularly John [Lennon], about this meeting and saying what a bad war this was. We started to investigate and American pals who were visiting London would be talking about being drafted. Then we went to America, and I remember our publicist—he was a fat, cigar-chomping guy, saying, "Whatever you do, don't talk about Vietnam." Of course, that was the wrong thing to say to us. You don't tell rebellious young men not to say something. So of course we talked about it the whole time and said it was a very bad war. Obviously, we backed the peace movement.

POWER: You were a megaphone for a generation.

McCARTNEY: People often say to me, "Do you think music can change the world?" and I do, on a lot of levels and one of those levels is just the fact that famous musicians are listened to.

POWER: So behind the image of wild, rebellious young men was a growing sense of responsibility?

McCARTNEY: That's right. We thought of ourselves as just sensible young people. We didn't think we were especially wild. There were millions of people, we were part of a movement. We weren't the worst by a long shot. We were rather innocent. Perhaps in terms of responsibility we did sow some seeds for people who came after. People like Geldof, Bono, people who have the megaphone now.

POWER: Did you contribute to social progress?

McCARTNEY: In an innocent way, almost unintentionally, I think we made a contribution. I think there is a certain freedom inherent in the whole Beatles thing. I get people now coming up to me wherever I am in the world, particularly America, saying, "You changed my life" and I think I know what they mean. When we first went, America was football jocks and crew cuts and I think there is less of that now.

POWER: But is there a darker side to progress? The Beatles contributed to the loosening of social constraints and that has left many people floundering.

McCARTNEY: I don't know. It's a strange argument. I tend to believe that people will sort of self-regulate, so that it's good to give them freedom.

POWER: But some people need clear signposts, especially the less well educated. For many the 1960s was a liberation, for others it was a long dark night.

McCARTNEY: Well, you cannot give freedom just to one small bunch of people and not to everyone. It's, of course, a question of balance. It's like with children: you want to give them space to run, but at the same time you want to give them structure and discipline. You want them to see for themselves that discipline is quite a good thing. I think it's always worse when people don't have freedom, just think of pre-freedom Russia — you couldn't think, buy a Beatles record, enjoy music. But people can abuse freedom. Things can grow too wild. The ivy can cover the house and wreck it. You have to do a bit of husbandry, that is what civilisation is really.

POWER: Going back to the 1960s we should remember how culturally stifling the atmosphere was. I have just read a book about Rudolf Nureyev, and how he was dancing with Margot Fonteyn at Covent Garden and in the interval ran outside to the men's public toilet, found somebody there, had a quick one and was running back when a policeman arrested him.

McCARTNEY: Brian Epstein, our manager, was gay or queer, as you would have called it then, not being derogatory. We were aware, because we had talked about it with him — he was a good mate to us — that if he was ever caught it meant jail. Again, that made us think why? Even in private, if you want to do that what does it have to do with anyone else?

POWER: If my memory serves me right, you never made a stand for homosexuality at that time.

McCARTNEY: It just never came up. Nobody ever said "what do you think about gay rights?" I think if they had said it we would have said it's a good idea.

POWER: Back home at that time Britain was seized with all sorts of troubles: there was a sense of decline, a stagnant economy, there were strikes all the time and lots of people were saying, "There are the Beatles and all this musical life in London, but the British are just dancing on the deck of the Titanic."

McCARTNEY: It was not something we felt we could do anything about. We were doing our bit for the economy by creating exports. If there are big problems, it's better to dance than just sit around and add to the problems. Your energy can affect other people.

POWER: In our lifetime we had the Cold War and then its sudden end — that's when we should have been out dancing on the streets. But there was this lack of passion; it ended in a whisper not a bang.

McCARTNEY: I wouldn't say it went unnoticed. I remember it with great joy. Anyway, the quote is ending in a whimper not a whisper.

POWER: Ah, the boy got an A in his A-level English!

McCARTNEY: I got my A, yes. Thanks to Alan Durband, our English literature teacher. He was a great teacher. I think he was the one who sat us together.

POWER: He was the one who singled you out, he made you head of our class and said, "Look, no messing around with Power, McCartney, it's only six weeks before the big exams." By the way what are you reading now?

McCARTNEY: The Dalai Lama's The Universe in a Single Atom. Did I ever tell you that I wrote to him once? He had written that, "As Buddhists we believe in not causing any suffering to any sentient beings." Then I found out he was not a vegetarian, so I wrote to him saying, "Forgive me for pointing this out, but if you eat animals then there is some suffering somewhere along the line." His reply is in one of my safe places, which means I have probably lost it! In Buddhism, you aren't meant to get too attached to anything, not even the Dalai Lama's reply! Anyway, he replied saying that his doctors had told him he needed it, so I wrote back saying they were wrong.

POWER: We have both lived through the coming to life of the Third World. At school we used to think of the masses of underfed people out there. Now these places are throbbing — Indonesia, India, Brazil, China. Even Africa is on the way up — if the current crisis doesn't undermine it. Do you get a sense that the world is making progress?

McCARTNEY: Yes, I do, slowly but surely.

POWER: Will our generation leave the world better than we found it?

McCARTNEY: I don't know about that, but what I do know is that our customs and habits need some quite severe restrictions to save the environment. Industrialisation in India and China is going to create a lot of problems — I once met the minister for the environment of India and he said, "We are about to enter the hole you are just getting out of." But I do feel that spiritually we are moving somewhere. Through mass communication, through the internet and so on, I think the idea that people are the same everywhere is starting to pervade our consciousness and that makes me optimistic. But that doesn't guarantee a benign future. I suppose we have either the Blade Runner future where everything has gone horribly wrong, or you have an enlightened future with the UN becoming more important and people and nations realising that most humans are very similar animals and that we can work things out.

Did you know I was just in Israel playing a concert? I was warned off going there, and then warned off going into the Palestinian territories. But I hooked up with an organisation called One Voice,

192

which is half-Palestinian, half-Israeli, they are working for peace, still hoping for a two-state solution. Their feeling is that it's not far-off, it's just hard for the politicians to sign off on it. I met some of them in Tel Aviv. I hadn't realised how intrusive the Israeli state is—if you want to do something like import a car into the Palestinian territories you have to get a permit from Israel. And a man coming to work in Israel has to start queuing at 3am to get to work at 8am. Isn't it time that we knocked all that on the head like we have managed to do, apparently, in Ireland.

POWER: Do you see it coming in the next few years?

McCARTNEY: I was certainly very inspired by these people in One Voice. I went to visit a music school in Bethlehem. I needed to go into Palestine if I was going to play Israel with a clear conscience. Everyone in the band wore the One Voice badges. I think that young people on both sides will get there.

POWER: What about this enormous financial crisis? Has the US been caught out by its own greed?

McCARTNEY: I think there is some truth in that. This is why a lot of us hope for a change in US politics with the election of Obama. He is the man for the job. I was very impressed by his decision to work on the south side of Chicago after getting his degree rather than take a lucrative job on Wall Street. I'm so glad he won. I think he will make a great president.

POWER: As one of the richest men in the world what's it like to be caught in this meltdown?

McCARTNEY: I am not one of the richest men in the world. There are many, many people above me.

POWER: And you have not taken a bad hit?

McCARTNEY: I don't know. If banks go bust I am sure we are all going to be hurting, because that is where we keep our money. In the 1980s when I was being advised to "get debt, man, it's great" I just said, no. I don't trust that idea; my father said: "Neither a borrower nor a lender be." What has gone wrong is this idea of borrowing way beyond your means. I remember a while back hearing one minute that Donald Trump was bankrupt and then I heard he was building a fleet of new hotels, I remember thinking how could that happen? I guess he had people's confidence and they loaned him some more. In my case, right from the start my dad said it was not a good idea to buy a guitar on the never-never. You should wait until you could afford it. That is why my bass guitar is quite a cheap instrument.

POWER: Do you still use it?

McCARTNEY: I still use the same one, yes. There were two reasons why I bought the Hofner bass. One was that it was affordable, that was the main reason and the other was it was symmetrical for a left-hander, so it did not look odd. They did not make special left-handed instruments in those days.

POWER: You may not be one of the richest men in the world, but you are very rich. Have you ever thought about giving it all away, like Bill Gates?

McCARTNEY: I admire those guys. I think it's really great. But I have my own personality and my own way of doing things. I was taught as a kid that if you give you should do it modestly, so a lot of my philanthropic efforts are done quietly. A friend of mine once told me off for not giving enough. I said, "You don't know what I give. Let me tell you one or two things. When the tsunami happened I gave money. When my school in Liverpool needed money I gave it to them." I am asked daily for contributions. One Voice have a thing they want me to help with. That is more how I do it. I do not have a massive programme, a mission, because I am still writing songs, I am still making music. As I say, some of the best things that have happened to me have happened unwittingly and I rather like that idea. I think there is a strength in that idea. It does not put you too far above people. There is a danger of you looking like a man with a mission; it starts to separate you from people. So, it is an interesting idea—to spend my time giving money away-but I am an artist and there is a slight difference.

POWER: You must allow space for inspiration.

McCARTNEY: There has to be a big empty bit in my head that tunes can fall into.

POWER: In 300 years' time there is a good chance that your stuff will still be sung and played. Does that give you a kind of awed feeling?

McCARTNEY: Yes. That gives me a great feeling. Even when that happens now, if I am in New York and, as happened recently, a black trucker leans out of his truck and says, "Hey, Paul, Let it be!" that thrills me. When we were kids, who would have imagined, in our dusty Alan Durband classroom that we would be here? That I would be sitting in my own office in London…

POWER: How could you imagine we were going to have such a rich life and I would be sitting here with the greatest pop star in the world, the guy I played cricket with in the school yard.

McCARTNEY: Americans would say "awesome." Let me tell you a little story to finish with. I was on a holiday recently in Long Island where I have a little sailboat and this nice lady lets me keep it on her beach. I just sail out very quietly on my own in the boat — me, the wind and the sail; it is a great balance to my high visibility life. As I was setting the boat up there was a group of guys just down the beach and I heard them singing. It was a quiet beach; there was nobody on it except me and them. I was just there staying with my girlfriend. I listened and it sounded so tuneful that I approached, and as I got closer I realised it was my song "Eleanor Rigby" they were singing. I just stood there until they finished and it was great, it was a beautiful arrangement — they turned out to be the Princeton Glee club. And when they finished I applauded them and said, "Can you imagine me as a kid in Liverpool, someone telling me that there would be an a cappella group of young men singing one of my songs on a beach in Long Island in America? It's uncanny."

POWER: I remember you telling me once that "Eleanor Rigby" was influenced by Alan Durband.

McCARTNEY: Yes, in a roundabout way. It was through the passion he instilled in us for the unlikeliest things, like Chaucer. For a 16, 17-year-old Liverpool boy, it is not easy to break through that barrier and get into Chaucer. And the passion he instilled in us definitely found its way into my songs. I think something like "Eleanor Rigby" owes a debt to Durband because I had seen structure, I had seen words put together in a nice order. He was taught by FR Leavis at Cambridge. I had never heard of Leavis, but I remember there was a Housman poem that we rather liked, but Durband insisted it was "sentimental old rubbish" and he said that came from the Leavis influence. So there is me getting this Leavis-Durband lineage. Durband gave me clues. For instance, he told me to read "The Miller's Tale," which was off-syllabus. He said, "They don't want you to look at this stuff, but you should have a look."

POWER: It is full of farts and fucks.

McCARTNEY: Yes, the woman famously puts her arse out the window and she says, "Give me a kiss, my love," and he says, "What is this, a beard?" Well, that floored me. And I thought OK, now you have got me. I think we were very lucky to go to that school.

POWER: You kept in touch with Durband?

McCARTNEY: Yes. He retired to Spain and died a couple of years after. He was a lovely man.

POWER: Did you ever tell him the story about the pedigree of "Eleanor Rigby"?

McCARTNEY: No, but I'm not sure I knew then. It's the sort of thing you only notice when you look back.

Chapter 14
The Press needs a big Reformation

A famous Fleet Street press lord once pinned up a notice in his paper's newsroom. It read: "One Englishman is a story. Ten Frenchmen is a story. One hundred Germans is a story. One thousand Indians is a story. Nothing ever happens in Chile." Why is it that the press, by and large, is still so inept at finding a way of presenting historical relevant facts, including the backwaters and the undercurrents? Why does it give so few of its resources to anticipating events? Why did UPI, the news wire, in February 1962 not have a single dispatch from Chile? Yet in the Chilean press it was reported that month that a Chilean had become the youngest cardinal in history (perhaps indicating Vatican perception of the coming revolt among young clergy in Latin America); and inflation had reached such a point that banking transactions were practically suspended. The shortage of clippings on this affair no doubt in part accounted for the lack of depth in much Western reporting on the final Salvador Allende economic crisis when, with CIA help, the democratically elected Marxist president was deposed by the army.

Chile/1962, which nobody thought important, is in fact a critical element for understanding Chile/2022, which elected once again a very left-wing president. And so it is with a multitude of other issues — energy, food, raw materials, racial and ethnic conflict — issues whose jagged peaks too often rise out of the clouds taking us unaware. Perhaps the most significant journalistic 'oversights ' in recent history has been the energy crisis combined with global warming, and in particular the events that led up to them; and the war in Ukraine where no one has ever explained to the public why the Russians rightly had considered Ukraine as part of Russia, and had so for over 500 years,

Our media today are blunt instruments in culling out the news that is important and lasting. Too often it is obsessed with a big shock event—as with the Russian/Ukraine war—or with the passing trivia of a dramatic moment—the Oscar 'slap'. Too often they are unable to pick out the particles that will later coalesce like globules of quicksilver into a mass—tangible and significant. They rarely have any sense of history. How many reporters or editors have a workable knowledge of the events at the end of the Cold War when President Ronald Reagan promised President Mikhail Gorbachev that if the two parts of Germany were allowed to unite "Nato would not expand eastward one inch". The continuous expansion of Nato provoked the Russian bear in its most vulnerable parts. If the press had educated its public on the history of events, then maybe Westerners would not have rushed so blindly to encourage Ukraine in its near suicidal fight.

News reporting, which is so wedded to the sudden, the jerk, the sharp break in continuity, finds it difficult to report the incremental, the casual, the imperceptible shifts in the affairs of man that cumulatively more often than not shape life on our planet.

The first indications of an energy crisis to come did not begin with the Yom Kippur war 1973 and the subsequent oil embargo against the West led by Saudi Arabia, resulting in a 300% price rise, although for our television channels this provided the first moving picture of the 'crisis'. It began in the early 1960s when OPEC was an infant yet was able even then successfully to resist price cuts by the major oil companies. Despite the warning signals, the media tended (there are always exceptions) to overlook the size of the changes underway.

Journalists can share the blame with the highly compartmentalised way intellectual pursuit is managed in our society. We journalists have always prided ourselves on being generalists, on having the virtue of being able to operate untrammelled by discipline or convention. We work across the board, pursuing leads wherever they might take us. Yet often in practice the generalist's argument is a defence for fickleness. By generalists we don't necessarily mean floating across intellectual demarcation lines or going back into history to make hard, succinct, well-researched, original, points about octopus-type problems. Rather we interpret generalism to mean flexibility in the face of diverse ever-changing news.

But why should our media be so limited, so inexpert? Why does the press insist on devoting so much of its time and talent to reporting the ephemeral, the trivial and the dramatic? Why is its bias, with occasional notable exceptions, against plumbing the depths?

In 1922, Walter Lippmann, the New York Herald Tribune columnist (often referred to as the greatest journalist of the twentieth century), published his landmark study "Public Opinion". He wrote that "News and truth are not the same thing and must be distinguished". Lippmann went on to argue that "The function of news is to signalise an event, the function of truth is to bring to light the hidden facts, to set them into relation with each other and make a picture of reality on which men can act." But should we accept this dichotomy between news and truth? Maybe in 1922, when people were less educated and newspaper staff less equipped to deal with issues intelligently, Lippmann's observations were a sad reflection on the inevitable. But today this dichotomy needs no longer hold sway; it is not a necessary and unavoidable one. Journalists in the top serious newspapers in the US and Germany have PhDs (less so in the UK). If they worked at it hard, as they did for their degrees, the contemporary quality and historical depth would improve quite dramatically.

Take the BBC as an example. At the time of the Brexit debate the BBC did make a strong effort to be impartial. But that's not quite the point. Impartial is a very slippery word. ("When I use a word Humpty Dumpty said, in rather a scornful tone, "it means just what I choose it to mean—neither more nor less." "The question is," said Alice, "whether you can make words mean so many different things.")

The internal Brexit debate by BBC editors on BBC output and whether it was biased had too many moments of great simplicity—a mere counting of heads on both sides. Of course, that's easier done than to pursue what is inevitably a subjective quest to balance the intellectual quality of the arguments made by the protagonists (as would be done in university exams).

What was missing in the BBC's output was history and the perspective derived from it. That is where the debate should have centred, not on the details of fishery, transport and Treasury policies or the issue of the degree of British influence in Brussels. There was little coverage, over the years, on the history of Europe and how and why the EU had created arguably the greatest buffer, in the history of humanity, against war. Few editors and reporters knew much about the history of the evolution of Europe since Charlemagne's time, or details of the Versailles Treaty at the end of the First World War, or the path-breaking Aland islands' (they lie in the Baltic Sea) ruling by the League of Nations. The way this dispute between Finland and Sweden over the ownership of the islands was solved is a template both for the Brexit debate and, also, for Russia/Ukraine today. The League's arbitrators, made up of very wise and experienced people, not populist newspapers and politicians, decided that Finland could keep its historical hold on the Aland islands despite its people wanting to become part of Sweden, as long as it placed no troops or armaments on its soil. This ruling is regarded as one of the defining moments of international law.

A similar criticism can be made today about the BBC's coverage of China and Russia. Most editors at the BBC news department were late teenagers when the curtain on communism in the Soviet Union came down. They know little of Gorbachev's arguments in favour of keeping the Soviet Union intact (which would have avoided the wars in Ukraine, Chechnya, Georgia, Ossetia, Armenia and Azerbaijan), and the chaos of the Yeltsin years and the early economic and social progress of the Putin regime which made Putin extraordinarily popular. They know little about the 500 years of Russian rule of Ukraine (and only 30 years of independence). They know not much about how the US and Nato broke their promise to Gorbachev not to expand the borders of Nato and how this provoked Putin and most Russians into thinking their country was being besieged. These editors set their agenda based on very short-lived memories and, too often, shallow historical knowledge. Moreover, they belong to the news school — "if it bleeds, it leads".

During the Ukraine war the big English-language papers, The New York Times, The Washington Post, The Wall Street Journal, The Financial Times, The Guardian and The Times have maintained a de facto embargo on printing opinion pieces that argued Gorbachev's (and Putin's) side and opposed the necessity for supporting Ukraine.

Mort Rosenblum, former editor in chief at the International Herald Tribune, in his book, "Coups and Earthquakes", comes up with a handful of sensible reforms which even in the budget-tight world of the 2020s could achieve results. He does not call for more editors or correspondents. Rather, better motivation and direction for those already there. Newspapers and TV channels should save their reporters for the difficult stories and let the agencies provide secondary local stories. He quotes approvingly a memo written by Seymour Topping when he was foreign editor of the New York Times, "We can be less preoccupied with the daily official rhetoric of the capitals. We should report more about how the people live, what they and their societies look like, how their institutions and systems operate . . . Our readers must have more sophisticated interpretive writing."

But how to get this higher quality, more analytical, reporting? I have a few suggestions. First—the way journalists are selected. The intellectual quality demanded of journalists must be improved. In many countries the media are finding it more difficult to attract the calibre of people they need. Not least is the problem of unionisation. In Britain, for example, the National Union of Journalists insists that journalists work themselves up the totem pole, often starting with a provincial rag—for that is what too many of them are. One has to have an unusual sense of dedication to take this arduous and unstimulating route.

Second—the question of age. Journalism is too often regarded as a young man or woman's profession. Unless one starts to climb the totem pole in one's early twenties, entry is difficult. Yet if journalism could adapt itself to hiring writers who have gained knowledge and expertise in other fields, that would enable a remarkable and steady transfusion of talent.

A third reform would be to allow writers and reporters to specialise more. For even when the media allow specialist reporters, news editors still expect their ' specialists' to concentrate on what they regard as hard news. Moreover, they expect them to submit copy nearly every day, or if it's a weekly, every week. So involved is the journalist in chasing ephemeral hard news, he or she has little time to read — journalists don't read much whether it be non-fiction or novels or to meet experts in universities for reflective conversation.

My fourth reform is the question of presentation. For once the decisions have been implemented to make sure that reporting attracts the best brains, once we give those brains time to be thoughtful and pursue the linkages, it is no use if editors play their output down by shunting the material to remoter parts of the paper or produce programs at times of the day which only the dedicated watch.

As important is the use of the front page or the lead item on TV and radio. The front page and the lead story are a paper's and station's most precious commodity. They help set the nation's agenda. Yet if that page or the news headlines are half given over to the announcement of presidential candidacy, a plane crash, a sudden rise in petrol (gas) pump prices, the inconvenience of a train strike, or more fighting in Ukraine and Syria, this potential is greatly reduced. Often, we have to ask, where is the depth in any of these stories?

When in the days of apartheid the Guardian (a serious UK paper with a sophisticated readership) a few years ago decided to lead on its front page with the story of the wage levels of South African black workers it created a furore whose course took a long time to run. A parliamentary committee was established. The cabinet, both in Britain and South Africa, discussed it. And in many cases wage levels moved dramatically upwards. However, it was not a new story. The essential facts had been known for decades. Yet its presentation was such as to force the issue to the top of the agenda.

Rosenblum concludes wisely: "A democracy cannot function without an informed electorate . . . Foreign policy cannot be left unchecked to a Washington elite, to specialists or to interested lobby groups. World crises, if foreseen in time, sometimes can be avoided. But without reliable reporting from abroad, citizens are vulnerable and weak".

It doesn't have to be like that. It's not just Walter Lippmann who has shown a better class of journalism. One thinks of the foreign affairs columnist, the late William Pfaff, my colleague at the International Herald Tribune and David Gardner, the Financial Times's Middle East editor who died last year. I myself have tried to live up to the standards I have outlined in this chapter.

It will be a tough fight to lead reform in the media world. Old habits are very much ingrained. We need not just reform here and there. The media needs a total Reformation. Then we can, step by step, progress to a state of Enlightenment.

Chapter 15
My most important two hour interviews

Zbigniew Brzezinski, President Jimmy Carter's
national security advisor and Georgi Arbatov,
Mikhail Gorbachev's chief foreign policy advisor

(Both reprinted from London's Prospect magazine.) Others which
are not reprinted here: Indira Gandhi, prime minister of India,
Sonia Gandhi, president of the Indian National Congress, Julius
Nyerere, prime minister of Tanzania, Olusegun Obasanjo, president of Nigeria, Ignacio "Lula" da Silva, president of Brazil, Cardinal Paulo Evaristo Arns of Sao Paulo, Chancellor Helmut
Schmidt of Germany, Chancellor Willy Brandt of Germany, Andrew Young, chief of staff of Martin Luther King, President Pervez
Musharraf of Pakistan. AND OTHERS. Most of these were printed
in The International Herald Tribune at broad sheet length.

Behind the interviews

Reflections on my visits to Moscow and Washington to visit two of the leading lights of the cold war

The stereotype of pre-revolutionary Russia lives on — a despotic tsar, a serf economy that lived long after the abolition of slavery by the Europeans (but not the Americans), and a malign, primitive, Asiatic influence rooted in the savage conquest by the Mongols and the Tartars.

But as the great historian of Europe, Norman Davies, has written, "[Late imperial Russia] was Europe's chief source of agricultural exports... Russian aristocrats, merchants, artists and professors were thoroughly integrated into every aspect of European life... Politically, Russia was thought be making serious liberal progress after 1905."

War with Germany threw Russia off the rails. But now it is back on them, where is Europe? When I put this question to Georgi Arbatov in Moscow last year, I could see him wring his hands with despair as he answered. When, in Washington DC a couple of months later, I asked Zbigniew Brzezinski more or less the same question, he answered that he thought that there was a real possibility that Russia would be invited into the EU within 20 years, but he also seemed to imply that in Yeltsin's time, a blinkered western leadership meant that a great opportunity had been lost to bind Russia closer into the west.

One of the joys of Moscow today is the seemingly infinite number of small, restored Orthodox churches, with their golden domes pointing skywards. Nearly every time I poked my head in, people were praying, often a choir singing or a priest dispensing incense. Russia in fact is the inheritor and guardian of the part of the Christian church that the Roman emperor Constantine moved to Constantinople when he made it the capital of his empire and the founding seat of Christian power.

In 1204, when the 1,000-year-old Christian capital was sacked—by Christian armies from the west—it led to the rooting of Orthodox Christianity among the Slav peoples (although Christianity had arrived in Russia over two centuries earlier). When the Ottomans finally captured Constantinople in 1453, the Orthodox church became the heritage of Russia. A Muslim Russia would have meant a very different history for the west. A Christian Russia means it is an integral part of European civilisation.

The Reformation and the Enlightenment never deeply penetrated Russia. The tsar wielded a kind of power that the rulers of Britain and France could only dream of. Yet the greatest of them, Peter, used that power to do what Atatürk later did to Turkey—give Russia a westernised makeover.

The EU must, once the war in Ukraine is over, pick up the unfinished business of modernising and stabilising Russia that ended in 1914. This is far more important—and should be more natural—than any of its other far-flung ambitions.

Many will say it is too late: Russians have already retreated into their nationalistic shell. I well understand their reaction. I saw the same response in Turkey after Europe started to backtrack on its promise of EU entry two years ago. Before that point, Turks were becoming more enthusiastic pro-Europeans by the year. A welcoming light by Europe would turn Russian opinion around. The Russians and Turks, both of them, need to be able to see that European green light. But with the war in Ukraine going at full blast this is highly unlikely for the time being.

My trip to Washington to visit my old sparring partner from the Carter days, Zbigniew Brzezinski, was more mind-blowing than my journey to Moscow, perhaps because I was seeing everything through the eyes of my 17-year-old daughter, Jenny, who was making her first trip to America. The things she wanted to see surprised me. I took her to the Lincoln memorial to show her the steps where Martin Luther King Jr made his "I have a dream" speech, but she made me walk the length of the Mall to look at the Vietnam war memorial. Instead of the eagles and rifles, as with older war memorials, all we saw were stark slabs of black marble with names of the American dead on them. As Michael Mandelbaum has written, "It represents the soldier not as hero but as an innocent and literally faceless victim." I was left to wonder how they will fashion the war memorials of Jenny's generation. Is there anything left to say after Vietnam? Will America ever learn in the way Europe has through its two horrific 20th-century experiences? Let's see how it will handle the countries and places militarily active in the aftermath of the Iraq war — Iran, Yemen, Gaza, Lebanon and Iran. Thus far, rather badly.

During the cold war, Brzezinski was a hawk among hawks, albeit an exceedingly clever and, in many ways, sensitive one who never underestimated man's spiritual needs in the materialistic fight between godless communism and consumerist, selfish capitalism. But he also had a propensity for political adventure — hence the famous photo of him peering down the Khyber Pass through the sights of a machine gun some months after the Soviet invasion of Afghanistan. Later, if not exactly a dove, he became America's most articulate critic of Bush's and Trump's warmongering.

Zbigniew Brzezinski remained almost to the last (he died 7 years ago) the feisty, acerbic figure he was when he served as President Jimmy Carter's national security adviser between 1977 and 1981. Back then he was seen as the man who gradually dissuaded Carter of his more pacific convictions. Brzezinski was responsible for the administration's confrontational tone over the Soviet Union's human rights failings. He argued within the White House for arming the Afghan mujahedin to fight the Soviets, even before the Red Army invaded. He had an important advisory role in Barack Obama's presidential campaign, and he emerged as President George W. Bush's most searing foreign policy critic. I met him this time in Washington to discuss the cold war, Putin's Russia, Iran and US foreign policy.

JONATHAN POWER Was the end of the cold war a missed opportunity?

ZBIGNIEW BRZEZINSKI In the Yeltsin era we could have done more to engage and perhaps entangle Russia in a relationship with the west, which might have reduced the nostalgia for imperial status that the Kremlin displays today. But it is an open question whether Russia was ready for it. This was a period of great confusion, of uncertainty and humiliation, so it might not have been easy to fashion something that would have lasted.

JP Was Nato expansion a good idea?

ZB I think it was a necessary idea. One can easily imagine the tensions that would dominate central Europe today in the absence of Nato membership. Look at the friction between Russia and Estonia, and at the threats, embargoes, even military gestures that Russia has been employing against Georgia and Ukraine. Clearly membership of both Nato and the EU has created a more stable and potentially co-operative relationship between central Europe and Russia.

JP Didn't James Baker [President Bush senior's secretary of state] make a commitment to Gorbachev not to expand Nato?

ZB I believe there was a commitment not to deploy Nato forces in eastern Europe—but not any explicit commitment that Nato would not be expanded.

JP Is there a danger that Russia might become a military adversary once again?

ZB I doubt it. For one thing, to be a military adversary of the US on a global scale, Russia would have to have some sort of mission, an ideological cause. That strikes me as unlikely. Beyond that, Russia's capabilities are far lower that they used to be. Russian society expects more for itself in socioeconomic development, and it is more difficult to deny it in the context of the relatively easy access Russians now have to the outside world. This recent posturing by Putin is a kind of childish machismo. It delays Russia's eventual association with the west. But I don't think Putin has done anything that gives cause for serious worry.

JP Was it a mistake after the end of the cold war not to bind Russia into a closer relationship with the EU?

ZB More could have been done to create a greater sense of identification between Russia and the west, particularly in the Yeltsin era. But it is an open question whether Russia as a society was ready for it. This was a period of great confusion in Russia, of considerable humiliation; it might not have been easy to fashion something that would have lasted in the long run. However, more should have been tried in the early 1990s.

JP Do you think that Russia is an integral part of western civilisation?

ZB Yes, as is Ukraine.

JP You can't compare Ukrainian writers, poets, composers or painters with the greats of Russia.

ZB That's not the issue. The question is: which society is more European? The Ukrainians have shown great ability to deal with diversity without recourse to arms. The Russians have a much greater propensity to solve problems by force. But both societies partake of the Christian heritage — which in turn is very much connected to the European heritage.

JP Would you like to like to see both those countries inside the EU within the next generation?

ZB I have often said if Ukraine moves to the west and becomes a member of the EU and Nato, Russia is far more likely to follow suit.

JP So it should be an ambition of the EU to aim for Russian entry, on certain conditions, within say the next 20 years?

ZB That is perhaps too soon, but the pace of history has certainly accelerated. I have given speeches about a Europe that extends from Portugal on the Atlantic to Vladivostok on the Pacific. When that will happen I do not know. However, if Ukraine is prevented from moving to the west, or is excluded, Russia's involvement with the west will be much more delayed, and there will be a higher probability of a nostalgic attempt at imperial restoration.

JP What do you think will be the consequences of Dmitri Medvedev becoming president of Russia and Putin his prime minister? Apart from anything else, is Medvedev too young and inexperienced?

ZB The whole arrangement is a constitutional farce. In any case, you could say that Putin was too young and inexperienced when he became president.

JP Both superpowers still maintain a formidable arsenal of nuclear weapons. How can the momentum towards nuclear disarmament be restored?

ZB By stopping proliferation. That's essential.

JP I thought big power disarmament was essential to create leverage on the would-be proliferators.

ZB Up to a point. But most proliferators are doing it not because they plan to engage in war with either the US or Russia but because of designs against a neighbour or fears of neighbours. I don't think we can contemplate a halt to the existence of nuclear arsenals without getting proliferation under control.

JP Surely there will be no credibility in dealing with the likes of Iran until there is a greater degree of nuclear disarmament by the big powers. Why do the big powers need these massive stockpiles?

ZB That is a fair debating point, although in reality we know that there is not going to be massive American and Russian disarmament. But despite the recent intelligence estimate that Iran ceased its nuclear programme in 2003, there is a concrete problem with Iran. With luck, in the next few years, progress will be made with Russia and America. But if we decide that we must wait for great-power disarmament for a resolution to the Iran problem, we are more likely to end up with a nuclear-armed Iran.

JP In your latest book, Second Chance, you are very critical of Bushes junior and senior, and of Clinton.

ZB Bush senior had a unique opportunity to resolve one major regional problem and to set in motion a bilateral solution to another. The regional problem was the middle east. Bush didn't exploit to the full the opportunities he had after the expulsion of Saddam from Kuwait, particularly in regard to the Palestinian-Israeli problem. Second, while he was effective diplomatically in dealing peacefully with the disintegration of the Soviet bloc, he didn't define any larger vision that might have captivated the Russian mind and given Yeltsin and his team greater confidence that they could be part of the west. To be fair, he may have been thinking of doing these things in a second term. Clinton was too mechanistic and self-indulgent in terms of the national mood at a time of great opportunity. But we should remember that the US electorate voted for a Republican congress which proceeded to reduce taxes on the rich and made American commitment to the global commonweal more rhetorical than real. My chapter on Bush junior is entitled "Catastrophic leadership." His was a truly appalling distortion of reality, which was demagogically propagated in order to mobilise US support for an unnecessary war. And in my mind there is a risk that the scope of that war may be enlarged even before Bush's departure.

JP In what sense?

ZB In the sense that the continuing conflict in Iraq could easily lead to collisions, flashes, provocations, a clash with Iran, perhaps some terrorist act in the US that can credibly be blamed on the Iranians.

JP If Bush's successor were a Democrat, how would you advise him or her to halt this?

ZB I would urge the president to take steps to bring the Iraq war to a political conclusion without delay. One, start talking to all Iraqi leaders, not just those in the green zone, about setting a date for American disengagement. That will focus Iraqi attention on dealing with their internal conflicts more responsibly. Two, approach all Iraq's neighbours for regional talks about assisting Iraqi security problems upon our departure. Every one of their neighbours, including Syria and Iran, has a stake in Iraq not exploding. And beyond that, try to engage other Muslim countries — Morocco, Egypt, Algeria — in assisting post-occupied Iraq. Three, ensure there's some major international effort, probably involving the UN, to undertake a rehabilitation of Iraqi society. And I would parallel the foregoing with a more serious effort to negotiate with the Iranians and with a more determined attempt to push Israel and the Palestinians to real peace, not an unsustainable armistice.

JP In an August 2007 article in Foreign Affairs, Barack Obama said the US must "lead the world once more." Surely, with the Bush era near its close, we've learnt that it doesn't work for America to lead the world alone. It has to be a group effort.

ZB Well, yes and no. The way I'd put it is that the US is, and potentially still will be, preponderant in foreign affairs. But one should not confuse preponderance with omnipotence. What "leading" really means is that the US is the critical catalyst for effective international co-operation. No one else can do it. There's a choice between leadership and domination.

JP The neoconservatives used 9/11 to put forward the notion that the US must use its power in a highly assertive way. Although the Iraq war has sobered the government, American foreign policy discourse is still well to the right of what it used to be.

ZB I'm not sure I agree. Yes, the neo-cons exploited 9/11. But I think that the reaction against the war means that the pendulum will swing back towards the middle. But it is hard to predict at what pace.

JP The nearest we ever came to a comprehensive peace deal between Israel and the Palestinians was under Clinton at Camp David, yet Ehud Barak's own foreign minister said that if he were Arafat, he would have rejected the proposals on offer as being too vague. How do you evaluate Camp David?

ZB I don't agree with you that they were the closest to success. I think Camp David 1 under Carter came much closer because something substantial followed — the first peace treaty between Israel and an Arab state, Egypt. It made possible the later peace treaty between Israel and Jordan, which means there's no possibility of a united Arab war against Israel. The Clinton-Barak-Arafat negotiations never came close to a breakthrough — the proposals were qualified to such an extent that it would have been very difficult for Arafat to embrace them wholeheartedly. I think he was clumsy in creating the impression that he was rejecting them, whereas in fact he was stalling. The American public didn't even understand that the negotiations continued after Camp David was over.

JP Let's return to Iran — the enmity goes back to your time, Carter's time. You made the mistake of letting your worries on the taking of hostages get blown up by the media out of all proportion. This was the root of the bad feeling between the US and Iran. Second, after the 1997 election in Iran, Clinton, fearing Israeli and Iranian lobbies at home, chose not to reach out to a more moderate Iranian president. The US has not played its Iranian cards cleverly.

ZB I think you are more correct in your diagnosis of the Clinton failure than in your emphasis on the hostage crisis. The crisis created a legitimate grievance for the US. The problem was the fall of the shah, and was related to something that at the time was not well understood — the legacy of the overthrow of Mosaddeq in the 1950s, which led over time to a US collision with Iranian nationalism. We were probably manipulated more than we realise by the British in the decision to remove Mosaddeq — his real quarrel was with the British. But after his overthrow, we stepped in on a large scale. We became the beneficiaries of the oil bounty, because the British did not regain their prominent position. Then we became the target of Iranian nationalism.

When the challenge to the shah arose, we procrastinated. We should have fished or cut bait much more quickly — either supporting the shah in an effort to repress the opposition, to prevent

Khomeini coming back, and then later embarking on reforms; or dumping the shah very quickly. Instead we tried to steer a middle course, which created ambiguity.

JP But you were the architect of that.

ZB I was one of the co-architects. I favoured the former course. Others favoured the latter. The combination of the two was not productive. We face the same dilemma now in Pakistan. We don't like a military dictatorship, but are we sure that populism, perhaps tinged with Islamic fanaticism, will be better?

JP Mitt Romney wrote recently that radical Islam's threat is "just as real" as that posed before by the Nazis and the Soviet Union. Isn't this attitude leading us down a dangerous path? It is a well-voiced opinion, not just in Republican circles but further afield among other influential Americans.

ZB It is a false narrative which capitalises on the historical ignorance of Americans. A candidate who says that either thinks, probably correctly, that the American people are ill informed — in which case he's being a demagogue — or he's stupid enough to believe it himself, in which case it offers a compelling argument as to why he should not be president.

JP How do you read China? There has been much talk lately about its increased defence expenditures and global ambitions.

ZB If we blow it, then China will probably become the most influential of those world powers that are not dominant. The Chinese — and I've dealt with them a lot — are patient, prudent and surprisingly well informed. They have an imperial tradition that allows them to take advantage of opportunities without overreaching. But they are not going to push the envelope in the foreseeable future. They have monumental domestic problems which we tend to underestimate. The reality is massively retarded infrastructure and a great deal of poverty.

JP You've said that America risks becoming a huge gated community, self-isolated from the world. What leads you to this conclusion?

ZB Surely you know what does. The question is: will it continue or get worse? That depends a great deal on what we've talked about. It also depends on whether there are further terrorist strikes in the US, and if so how the country, particularly the leadership, reacts. One of my indictments of Bush is that he has fostered a culture of fear rather than diminished it. I view the responsibility of leadership to be the fostering of confidence.

Georgi Arbatov

Death of Soviet Union's foreign policy guru —
my column of October 21, 2010

Georgi Arbatov, who died this month, was the Soviet Union's supreme two timer. On one side was the Soviet Union. On the other was the US. He spoke to them both, attempting to bring them together. He advised four Soviet leaders. When Mikhail Gorbachev took the top job he became his closest foreign affairs advisor. Gorbachev told his secretary that whenever Arbatov phoned she was to put him right through.

He wasn't exactly a chameleon but he was a fixture in US foreign policy circles where at the height of the Cold War he argued the case for détente, suggesting it was in America's interest as well as the Soviet Union's. The USSR, he maintained, was not hostile to the West and wanted to get out of the straitjacket of the Cold War. At times he could sound like an American liberal Democrat. Indeed, Senator Edward Kennedy was a friend and admirer.

He was a fixture on both Soviet and US television. He had a way in public of going right up to the edge of the red lines, but never quite crossing them. He had an unerring ability to watch his back. He knew that the other centre of power was the Soviet military-industrial complex. On one occasion he had an almighty row with Dmitri Ustinov, the head of the Soviet armed forces, about a new nuclear arms deal. He wondered afterwards if he had cooked his goose. But a week later Ustinov appeared on the doorstep of his modest flat to give him a bunch of flowers to celebrate his birthday. (Like his friend Yuri Andropov, Gorbachev's predecessor and boss of the KGB, he lived fairly simply, unlike most of the leadership.)

He records in his autobiography how when an agreement on a Strategic Arms Limitation Treaty had all but been completed

Brezhnev phoned Ustinov and hollered down the line for a good half hour. His voice was so loud that the US delegation said they could hear it right down the corridor where they waited. Ustinov buckled. By the time of Gorbachev, Arbatov had honed his skills to a sharp point. He formulated for Gorbachev the ideas that led to the end of the Cold War. He gave Gorbachev confidence in his diplomacy and negotiations with the US president, Ronald Reagan. (Gorbachev had not touched foreign affairs until he became General Secretary.) This led to a serious effort at total nuclear disarmament, made easier by Gorbachev's unilateral decision to ban medium range nuclear missiles in Europe—another of the Arbatov causes. He was as influential on Afghani policy. He was one of a small group who persuaded Gorbachev to withdraw the Soviet army of occupation. He had an abiding interest in Chinese affairs. In an interview with me in 1978, which I did for the International Herald Tribune, he told me if the West "pursued a closer relationship with China, turning China into some sort of military ally of the West". Then there would be "no place for détente". By issuing this threat Arbatov in effect demonstrated the long leash that Brezhnev gave him. At that time the Chinese-Soviet relationship was in the pits. Two and a half years ago—in his last full-length interview with a Western journalist—I asked him if he feared the present Chinese military build-up. He replied: "I don't see a clear and present danger.

For so long China was deprived of a place in the international community. It made an imprint on their psychology. Now they are involved in a real attempt to build their country. At the same time we have no guarantees that military people won't come to power. This will be bad for China and its neighbours."

In his book he is very critical of Gorbachev for not using his immense power to turn the Soviet Union into something like a social democratic state. "Having inherited awesome power that thrived on the fear ingrained in most of us since the horrors of Stalinism, he did not use that power for the public good." After a couple of years in power during which he was a force for liberation he steadily moved to the right surrounding himself with men who were later to try and overthrow him. In Arbatov's recent conversation with me he made many of the same points but then concluded that "Gorbachev was the best leader we ever had, even better than Andropov."

****

One warm day in August 2007 Georgi Arbatov, the éminence grise of the Soviet foreign policy apparatus, was waiting for me at the bus stop an hour out of Moscow. A little bowed at 84, he grabbed me by the arm and leant on his homemade walking stick, cut from a nearby birch, and led me through the wood I had arrived into a clearing in which stood a small, shabby block of flats, paint peeling in the entrance, a year's dust and leaves on the staircase. Like his mentor, Yuri Andropov, the former KGB chief and later head of the Soviet Union, Arbatov has always shunned many of the perks of the apparatchiks, content with a modest flat in the city and this "dacha" in the countryside.

We talked, as we did 30 years ago, over vodka, coffee, cucumber and beetroot. The adviser to every Soviet president from Brezhnev to Gorbachev remains as lucid as he was when he told me in 1978 that if the west pursued a closer relationship with China, turning China "into some sort of military ally to the west"... then there would be "no place for détente."

My full-page interview with Arbatov — which ran first in the International Herald Tribune, the Washington Post and later in many other papers (with a report on it on the front page of the New York Times and The Londoin Observer) — caused an enormous stir. It was the first time a senior Soviet official had talked at length to a western journalist on the record, without notes and answering every question put to him. Edward Crankshaw, the distinguished Sovietologist, described it in the Observer as "the most interesting thing to come out of official Moscow since the fall of Khruschev 14 years ago." The Economist made it its cover story.

We began our second talk with Stalin. Like Arbatov, I am convinced the in-built hostility of much of the western foreign policy elite towards the Soviet Union and later Russia has its foundations in a false reading of Moscow's post-second world war territorial ambitions. To understand today's deteriorating relationship, we have no choice but to begin there.

JP If you had died when you were 55, would you have been as at peace with yourself as you obviously are now?

GA I was very critical of many aspects of our way of life, but of course you couldn't speak about it. But I don't feel I compromised. Maybe I was fooled by these stupid ideological things we were saying all the time. But I felt the initiators of the cold war were the Americans. I think that the bombing of Hiroshima and Nagasaki were in reality the start of the cold war. In his memoirs, Henry Stimson, the American secretary of war during the second world war, says that it was done to teach the Russians to play according to the new rules of the game.

JP You don't think Stalin was planning a confrontation with the west after his victory in the war?

GA No. When Stalin met the French and Italian communist leaders, Maurice Thorez and Palmiro Togliatti, they asked for his advice, saying they had revolutionary situations in their countries and that it might be the moment to start a revolution. But Stalin replied, "Under no circumstances. It will not be tolerated by the west."

Stalin was an awful figure but he was a realist. He understood that his country was on the edge of a terrible future. People couldn't tolerate much more hunger. Every family had experienced the awful losses of the war.

JP But he was committed to an expansionist Marxist ideology.

GA Yes, he thought the victory of revolution was inevitable. But after the terrible war, he was afraid to start something new and dangerous. He preferred to wait and allow persuasion, the contradictions of the capitalist system and new economic crises to play their course.

JP In your book, The System: An Insider's Life in Soviet Politics, referring to the Soviet intervention in Angola and Afghanistan, you wrote: "Why did we in the eyes of the world become an aggressive expansionist power in the second half of the 1970s?" But you didn't really answer the question.

GA My guess is that the military-industrial complex had grown to such proportions that it escaped political control. The leaders depended on the military-industrial complex to stay in power. So they didn't want to estrange their relations with it. Not everything was controlled by one man.

JP Why did Gorbachev fail? Why didn't he use his immense power to push things forward faster?

GA Gorbachev was frightened to go forward because he wasn't sure that public opinion was ready for it. It was a pity. I consider him the best leader we ever had, even better than Andropov.

JP Yet in your book you are very critical of him.

GA It is because he didn't use his opportunities. And he allowed the Soviet Union to disintegrate. Three drunken men plotted it in the forest—Yeltsin, Leonid Kravchuk from the Ukraine and Stanislav Shushkevich from Belarus, in the Bialowicza forest. This meeting is well known, but the fact that they were very drunk is not so well known.

JP How do you know that?

GA I heard this from one of those present.

JP Are you prepared to say who this was?

GA No.

JP And what about the influence of the military-industrial complex in today's Russia? Has it been brought under control?

GA The economic difficulties of post-Soviet Russia made military expenditures much more modest, to the detriment of our security, but Putin is in the hands of this military-industrial complex, and a lot of his appointments go to these people. I don't know how much control he has over them. In general they have to worry about their survival in the military-industrial complex, not about enhancing peace.

It is very difficult to justify big military expenditures when the country is in so much need. I don't know Putin or the people around him — but looking from the outside, maybe he is afraid of being blamed for neglecting the needs of the military. The communists would blame him, Vladimir Zhirinovsky would blame him. You have a lot of adventurers now.

JP Has the west missed its chance of engaging Russia?

GA Was the end of the cold war really used by both sides? No. The US was infatuated by being the only superpower and started some adventures. Not all of them were bad. Kuwait was OK — it had to be done. But Iraq was just not well prepared, the intelligence agencies didn't do a good job, and it was not well executed. So now they are engaged in a bad war with a very doubtful outcome. Iraq can make America so tired that it will go away as happened in Vietnam.

Russia has also failed to respond properly to the end of the cold war, because of our internal problems. Our leaders were satisfied by being accepted as a member of the G8. I don't think another cold war is imminent, but we have entered into a period of multilateral international relations with many centres of power. We had this before the first world war. It is not easy politics. It demands a very big effort and a lot of brainwork. I'm not sure that both sides have prepared for this. We can slip into worse and worse situations, step by step.

JP So why has it become so bad? Why the decisions being made on arms control and troop control? Why the tense situation with Britain?

GA The main thing is that real negotiations have stopped. Both sides are at fault. They lose interest in each other.

JP If you were president of Russia today, what would you do to stop this situation?

GA I would start serious negotiations — two or three summits to discuss the new international situation, possible lines of behaviour and the responsibilities of big countries. We need negotiations all the time. If you do this, you become interested in the other country. You meet your adversary regularly and you get to know him. I know how the old summit meetings were. All organisations, including mine, were busy up to the ears. We had to work, work, work. Now they have lost interest. In my country the government has lost interest in consulting the academic community. I fear it is similar in the US. Now it just theatre, just show. They shake hands, a couple of photos, but no serious negotiations.

Now nobody is interested in anything. I have no idea where they get their information and ideas. Putin's is the least transparent governmental system in my memory. I don't know the people around Putin. What do they think? Medvedev? I don't know. He's not a public figure. He doesn't express himself.

Putin has done a lot of good work — he has re-established the governmental system. But at the same time he fails to explain himself. What are we striving for? What do we want to have in internal policy, in foreign policy? The average mental weight of people in power is falling. And you don't get to know them. It started with Yeltsin. On Sunday someone prompted a name. On Monday he named a new prime minister.

JP Are you worried that the west will once again start to consider Russia a military adversary?

GA It depends on what the Russians do. If they act like mad, then it is possible. But I don't think we will do it; the whole economic situation forbids it. You have seen, on the way here, these small towns with big, expensive houses. This is what the bureaucracy are interested in. They are not interested in work or war or confrontation or world revolution. You could send the police to any of these houses and ask them where they got the money. It is all dishonest money. There are no such salaries that allow you to buy such places.

JP Putin thinks the US took advantage of Russia when it was weak—the expansion of Nato, expanding influence into the old southern Soviet Union. Now Putin is fighting back, abrogating old agreements, threatening to re-target Europe with missiles.

GA I am not too worried. I'm more worried about what happens inside Russia. The new generation. What will it do? What will it think? They have no knowledge of the past and they seem uninterested in the future. It is just today's material needs. Tomorrow these young people will become important.

The other is the economic situation. We are so dependent on the high oil price, which will drop. I don't know how Putin will deal with it. We are like a drug addict, sitting on the needle of high oil prices.

JP I decided to come and see you today because we now appear to be entering a new dangerous phase—the ghosts of the past, after all, have not been laid to rest.

GA We have to stop this stupid talk about how Russia will go its own way. It's nonsense. The leadership must think more about where the present situation is leading the country, how to solve these problems and where exactly they want to lead the country to.

JP Why has the relationship with Britain soured so badly?

GA In the absence of real problems we have these kind of blown-up problems. The villains are Russian citizens who are here now but at the time were in Britain.

JP Is there a cover-up to protect the killers of Litvinenko?

GA It's very far from me and my work so I don't have the real picture. There may be a cover-up. There might be sheer stupidity—I know the quality of the people around Putin. This kind of thing is what I'm afraid of: small things that just appear, that haven't been planned before, but that have bad consequences.

JP Are you worried about poor control of Russia's nuclear arsenal?

GA We have had a lot of technical catastrophes, which makes the mass of weapons a dangerous thing.

JP But is the political climate benign enough to consider more cuts in nuclear weapons?

GA Both sides have lost their enemy. They see no imminent danger from the other side. Neither seems to understand that it can quickly reappear. Just the existence of so many weapons makes deteriorating relations more likely and stability less dependable.

If you have so many nuclear weapons, you have to say there is a plan to get rid of them even if you can't give the exact date. Otherwise, other countries say: if you have them, why can't we? Possession of nuclear weapons is now becoming a sign of a "great country." What enemies does North Korea have? None, but it wants to be great and mighty.

In the cold war days we were afraid that we would get into serious trouble because something bad was done. Now we must be afraid because neither side does anything good and just hopes things will go on like they do. But they will not simply go on. The situation is constantly changing. We can have new dictators appearing from nowhere who wish to have such weapons.

The blame for a lack of nuclear disarmament in the US and Russia must be shared equally. Being honest, we in Russia are not right in our approach. We could decrease our number of weapons unilaterally and show an example. We could dismantle our rockets and take others off alert, and the Americans would be obliged to follow us.

JP Who do you blame most for this on the American side, Bush or Clinton?

GA Bush has to be blamed more—because of his use of military force.

JP Do you think a new cold war is starting up?

GA It is not. But we can get into one. It'll be different—not ideological. It will be more difficult than the last one because we now live in a multipolar world with small states possessing nuclear weapons. Before, the US and USSR could control everyone; now everybody is becoming uncontrollable. I'm not saying we are, but we could be on the threshold of a more dangerous period than the cold war. Two years ago it was impossible to think of this. Now it is possible. Much will depend on the personalities of the future leaders of the US and Russia.

JP Who would you like to see become US president?

GA Hillary may not be a bad president. Barack Obama, I don't know him.

JP Obama said recently: the US "must lead the world once more."

GA If he wants to become leader, to command the world, then he is naive. Even if he thinks it, he shouldn't say it aloud.

JP Mitt Romney wrote that "Radical Islam's threat is just as real" as that once posed by Nazi Germany and the Soviet Union. "The consequences of ignoring this challenge—such as a radicalised Islamic actor possessing nuclear weapons—are simply unacceptable" he said.

GA They've found the lost enemy! Now everything can be explained and justified, military expenditure, military action, everything. A "war of civilisations" is quite artificial.

JP Will all this continue after Bush?

GA It will. We have to find a way among various Islamic leaders to negotiate because this is bad for Christianity and for Islam. We need maybe a conference of China, Japan, Malaysia, Indonesia, Egypt and some from the Christian world.

We must avoid a whole new generation growing up with this "war of civilisations" idea. It can become a self-fulfilling prophecy.

Pakistan has nuclear weapons. Iran may have them one day. We can stop this proliferation only in an improved climate brought on by the big powers reducing their own stocks. We should set the example and then say: why do you need them? Do you fear other countries? If you do, let's discuss it and see if we can help you find a way to negotiate.

JP Are you, like the Pentagon, worrying about a Chinese military build-up?

GA I'm not very at ease with the idea. It's more of a military threat to Russia than it is to the US. But I don't see a clear and present danger. China is doing rather well, in a peaceful way, by entering the world market.

For so long China was deprived of a place in the international community. It made an imprint on their psychology. Now they are involved in a real attempt to build their country. At the same time we have no guarantees that military people won't come to power. This will be bad for China and for its neighbours. Continuing negotiations with China is important. We have to build a multipolar international system and have to base our common security on this.

JP Do you think, like Gorbachev, that Russia should be part of the European "house"?

GA Of course. Russia has a lot to contribute to the EU. Why should it be kept outside, as Estonia and Poland want? That bad history has passed. If we lived only in the past, no one would shake the hand of a German. The EU has to help now, even symbolically — to make it clear that it is not against Russia coming into the EU. If the EU could say that in a decade or two Russia could enter, it would help stabilise Russian politics.

Note: The interviews with Brzezinski and Arbatov are reprinted from the leading UK intellectual magazine, Prospect. (The two earlier ones were published in The International Herald Tribune on October 10th 1977 (ZB) and November 21st 1978 (GA).)

END

Edition Noëma
info@edition-noema.de

www.edition-noema.de
www.autorenbetreuung.de